# HYPNOTIC AMNESIA

TO Emily —
from One Kindred Spirit
to another!

?

# BY LeeAllure AND D.J. Pynchon

**Dedications**
To the wonderful minds out there: the ones which are quick and facile, the ones which examine things thoroughly before they act, and the ones which proffer new ways of looking at, hearing, or doing things. —*LA*

To Mrs. Vanilla Pynchon, for her constant support in this, and all my odd endeavors. It means the world to me. —*DJ*

**Thank you**
Thank you to all the wonderful people who have assisted us in making this book a reality in some form, either by transcribing, proofreading, editing, contributing or supporting! Mrs. Pynchon, MattH, JohnE, JohnR, Ms Mesmer, Wiseguy and my own personal Michael Clayton.

**Important Disclaimers**
By reading and using the experiments in this book you are agreeing that you and your partner(s) are mentally healthy, proceeding carefully and that you agree only you are responsible for the ways in which you use these materials. This book is for informational and entertainment purposes only and should not be used for therapeutic purposes without the oversight or involvement of a licensed professional.

Hypnotic Amnesia
The Book You Remember on How to Forget

38 Spring Street, Box 1532
Nashua, NH 03061
www.hypnoticamnesia.com

ISBN 1517055369

ISBN-13: 978-1-5170553-6-3

## *Prologue*

What do you already know about how to forget? In what ways have you caused others to remember or forget things?

Most humans are pretty good at both of these, but doing it deliberately, through the use of hypnosis, is another story.

Perhaps you want someone you work with to do something very specific when they come home from work, and only remember that they've done it and because of you after the fact.

Perhaps you like the idea of being turned on by doing something, doing it, being turned on, forgetting all about it, and then being compelled to do the thing which caused that cycle in the first place, over and over, until some natural or specific end point. Maybe it's really hot for you to stand there, insisting that you won't do x, y, or z while you're doing it.

This book on Hypnotic Amnesia came about because it's something I was fascinated right from the beginning of my starting to do hypnosis. Some of my subjects automatically or instinctively didn't remember our sessions, and some did, but wanted not to.

I wanted to make sure that people I played with really were hypnotized, as opposed to role-playing. Having them not remember what we did in session, or doing something post-hypnotically that they were unaware of doing or surprised by doing seemed like a wonderful and fun thing to make happen.

My love for sharing amnesia techniques goes back to the first NEEHU* (New England Erotic Hypnosis Unconference) in 2010, when I taught a class on it there. I wanted to understand ways other people used amnesia in hypnosis, and what other ways there were for it to be caused.

DJ and I started discussions for this book in March of 2014, and did most of the experiments roughly in order, although we recorded Ms. Mesmer's Dual Inductions at MEEHU 1 in July 2014, the Esdaile State at DeepMindDarkWood 2014 and really played around with the Explosion during our Hypnotic Amnesia talk at MEEHU 2, July 2015. Many of the ideas we had came while we were working on my original list of twelve techniques, and we definitely jumped around the order a little, sometimes due to an experiment not working as we'd hoped, so we re-did them, or because we felt they would group nicely in a certain configuration. We've tried to make reference to where we fully explain most ideas, although it's possible some things have been missed. We appreciate your understanding and welcome your comments and questions for clarity.

This book is a conversation—between a hypnotist and a subject, between the hypnotist and the unconscious of the subject, and between the subject and his unconscious. Lee mostly uses an instant sleep trigger for DJ, and then goes onto suggestions. If you'd like inductions, we recommend *Mind Play* or *Mind Play, the Study Guide* by Mark Wiseman. They're meant for beginners to hypnosis, erotic or otherwise.

Who remembers what, who does what? How do we agree upon what is fun and sexy to do, and what makes us uncomfortable. How do we bump up against our own limitations and still continue on, what compromises and adjustments do we make?

This book is also a lot of hypnosis transcripts—of a hypnotist and her initially responsive subject, who gets more responsive and adept as we go along, capable now of waking trance states and even more fascinating ways to remember, to forget, to have memories adjusted or outright removed and replaced. The style of the spoken language has largely been kept so that perhaps you, too, can 'hear' me say these things as DJ did. You do not have to use my words, or my style, and you can still glean a lot of information from what I said and how I said them, to make these techniques work for you. You should be able to discern our process, how we came up with some of the later techniques, as you read through our discussions. We have also made some transcripts available through Amazon of the actual recordings we made of our sessions so that you can listen to pacing and responses.

You can use DJ's words and understandings to make yourself as a subject understand how and what's safe for you to forget, and what you might need to remember. You can know that it's OK for your unconscious mind to make sure that you only do the things you really want to, and to enlist its help in doing these things spectacularly well. You can use Lee's words, successes and failures, to understand that it's more about adjusting, picking up and going on again, to create powerful and positive experiences for your subject and yourself, than dwelling on failures.

As you go along, practicing both forgetting (and remembering!) on each side of the watch, you should become better at these skills. Use the worksheets to keep track of your progress. Join in the conversations at http://hypnoticamnesia.com to share what worked for you, what worked better, new ideas you have come up with regarding amnesia, fun experiments for others to play around with, fun 'kinky human tricks' with amnesia, and even participate in the community of other people interested in this topic.

Understand, as you read this book, that our success for all of this came about through *doing* these exercises, *communication* about what worked, what didn't, what felt good and what felt wrong. Then we let that information, that feedback, to work its way through how we then continued doing things, to how we still do things today, with an *awareness* of how amazing the unconscious is, how capable humans are, and *with respect* for each other as partners in this endeavor.

Thanks for reading, and remember—playing with amnesia can help to improve your memory—they're flip sides of the same coin.

LeeAllure
November 11, 2015

* EHU's are Erotic Hypnosis Unconferences, annual hypnosis conventions, or similar. NEEHU is held on the east coast, currently Hartford, CT in March, MEEHU is held in Chicago in the summer, WEEHU is held in the fall in San Francisco. Other events include DMDW, DeepMindDarkWood, held in Massachusetts in the fall and London Hypnosis Workshops, held in London in late winter.

# INTRODUCTION

## *Thoughts Pre-experiment*

### *Much Trepidation*
### *New light casts mental shadows:*
### *Would I lose my mind?*

DJ: Before we started our experiment, I sat down to capture my thoughts on hypnotic amnesia as a concept, and what I was expecting to get out of the experience. What follows is drawn from what I wrote at the time: As I sit to write this, I realize that this is kind of a confessional. As I sit to read it again later, I realize that it almost sounds crazy, after all the things I describe below, that I would still go ahead with this experiment. Yet this opportunity came at the perfect time for me; I had made a conscious decision in my life to embrace the things that scared me or put me off. This is one of those things.

When I was in eighth grade, one of the reading assignments was a novel called Flowers for Algernon. It's a very compelling book (and the movie, starring Cliff Robertson in an Oscar-winning performance, is really good). In the book, a mentally challenged man is experimented on with a drug that gives him super-human intelligence. The arc of the book is that, ultimately, the drug wears off, and he is deposited back where he started, with none of the capacities he once had. This story had a profound effect on me; it's why I didn't really experiment with drugs in college; and, ironically, it's why experimenting with hypnosis is so charged for me now. The novel brought alive a sense of the costs of losing something as precious as one's own intelligence. As I grew up and matured, this became conflated somewhat with my own issues involving loss of control. As someone who feels like he lives inside his head, and relies on his own brain-power for a living, mucking about with the brain, or memories, just seems like a terrible, terrible idea.

6

Compounding my worries about playing around with my brain, I had several incidents in high school where various people I considered my friends hid things from me in a way that made me feel humiliated. Looking back now, these incidents don't seem particularly important emotionally, but they do still crop up from time to time. Even today, I hate missing something; being in a room in which everyone else is in on the joke, but I'm not, is akin to that nightmare that others have of being naked in the middle of high school. One of the lessons I've been trying to learn through experimenting with hypnosis is letting go of those particular neuroses.

Taken together, my fear of losing intelligence with my fear of this particular form of humiliation, might seem to be an insurmountable challenge in terms of accepting hypnotic amnesia play. In fact, a question one might very well ask is, given these fears, why even bother? Part of it is to see if my brain can overcome those obstacles. I believe that it's important to face the fears that might hold you back. My guess is that the fear of losing my intelligence is rooted, in part, at my insecurity regarding whatever mental gifts I may have. Who would I be without them? Would I still be worthwhile? Would I still be, in a word, 'me'? My insecurity regarding humiliation is, likewise, rooted in my own self-regard, and need for appreciation from others. Under what circumstances can I let go of those fears? Hypno-amnesia may or may not be the way to do it, but I do believe that throwing myself into a research project (so to speak) regarding hypno-amnesia will poke and prod at the contours of those fears.

So what is hypnotic amnesia to me? Partly I've seen it in play with 'teleportation' experiments. I've seen it written about in some blogs and short stories. It seems to include everything from the classic hypnosis stage show trick that you can't think of your own name, or forgetting what city or state you're in, to full on freeze-frame. At least, that's how it seems from the outside. I think one of the more fascinating things about this topic is just how 'personal' it is as something to play with. Theoretically, a good actor can 'pretend' to be someone hypnotized to forget something and you couldn't know about it, as a disinterested observer. It's a tricky one to test if the subject is invested in a particular outcome.

For me, although it would be nice to have a brain which cooperates, and actually succeeds at hypnotic amnesia (and certainly it would be nice to therefore participate in writing this book), if I can't succeed, I don't think it would be a disaster for me; I don't have any major skin in the game, so to speak. But the larger point is that it would be me who is experiencing it; I wouldn't have to trust the evident experiences of other people.

So these are the stakes: is my mind willing to do this? Can I trust someone enough to give up access to my brain for the periods of time it would take to try this? How much would it change me? (Anything you experience changes you, so I knew something inside of me would change.) How will it happen? How much will it happen? And, do I have the talent to write about it effectively, authoritatively, and clearly?

Well, there's only one way to find out.

# CHAPTER ONE

## *Experiment 1 Forgetting to Remember and Remembering to Forget*

### *A good place to start*
### *Double binds of forgetting*
### *Basic, not simple.*

When we first came up with the list of possible methods to see how hypnotic amnesia would work for DJ, this use of what hypnotists refer to as a "Double Bind" was listed as the first experiment to try because it is, essentially, the most basic of the methods. A double bind in its simplest form presents the listener with a choice between two options. In day-to-day life, this is used all the time by salespeople ("Would you like to pay with cash or credit card?") or, if one wanted to be cynical, politicians ("Would you rather be taxed more or have more debt?"). The speaker has selected two options and presented them as a choice, essentially forcing the listener to choose from between only these two choices.

In hypnosis this can be used in a variety of ways. "Are you noticing first that your stress is melting away or that your eyes are getting heavy?" More subtly, it can influence the mind in a kind of Moebius Strip: "The deeper you go, the more you want to relax; the more you relax, the deeper you want to go."

In this context, the instruction is to "Forget to Remember, Remember to Forget" something. The double bind is to limit the mind to two choices, forgetting to remember and remembering to forget. That's the simplicity of the instruction. However, it wasn't quite simple in its execution, as the transcript makes clear.

LA:  So our intent is to start off with the easiest, not the easiest, I need to find a new name to call this, but our intent is to start off with the most mild of the suggestions and then to work up to the more sledgehammer-y suggestions. So certain people have abilities that are different from others and for some people when you say "Forget to Remember and Remember to Forget," that automatically happens but let's put you in a nice state of trance first and just see how effortlessly your unconscious mind takes you from here all the way down into deep sleep. *Snap!*

Then as your mind does that perhaps it's easier to tell your unconscious that's exactly what you'd like to have happen, that as we start to work on this hypnotic amnesia book, that it becomes useful to get into that mindset to be able to do that more and more easily.

And I'm also willing to bet that your unconscious mind is going to get to that place where it begins to, especially as we go through the different procedures that we've outlined, that it begins to get this idea of what's expected of it, and so we may not need the sledgehammer effects, but your mind may just get better and better at doing hypnotic amnesia for you. But in the meantime, let's think about this one particular phrase: remember to forget and forget to remember.

And as you think about what it means to remember to forget something it means you have an idea, you have a memory about something, about something in your head, and I don't know what just popped into your head right now but whatever that is perhaps you can find yourself remembering when you come out of trance to forget that you thought about it and forgetting to remember that you thought about it, and because I'm being repetitive, even though it is a mild suggestion, perhaps the idea that no matter what it was you were thinking about that remember to forget and forget to remember becomes exactly what you do. And it gets really simple to find yourself there. Now will you remember what it was that you were supposed to remember to forget and forget to remember? Or will your brain simply forget to remember, and you'll know there was something but you won't quite know what it was?

I don't want to actually tell you what to do other than forget to remember and remember to forget that there was something that popped into your head that now you've forgotten what it was and you're going to forget to remember what it was so that by the time you come out of trance you won't have remembered it at all and that's perfectly OK. Now we could go on to do all sorts of other things and perhaps I can give you something to think about that you'd find yourself forgetting, but I'd much rather not have your conscious self able to fixate on one thing. I want to save that particular thing for another time.

Come back on the count of five—wide awake, alert, remembering to forget what it was that popped into your mind, and absolutely forgetting to remember what it was that popped into your mind. And perhaps you'll forget to remember first or you'll remember to forget first, either one is OK. One, two, three, four, and five, wide awake.

DJ: Wow. I don't even know if I thought anything.

LA: Wait, so are you saying that, because you're not saying anything, that that was more effective than you expected?

DJ: Yes. That's exactly what I mean to say. I actually don't know if my brain thought of anything when you said to think of something.

LA: Would that surprise you because you're brain's pretty active, it probably thinks of a lot of things?

DJ: So much so that by the end my brain was thinking of something to put in that spot so I could say I had something I'd thought of.

LA: And what was that?

DJ: That was maybe a book but I don't have any recollection of anything I thought of that I forgot.

LA: So if I asked you to have something pop into your head does it?

DJ: Yes.

LA: And if I ask you to have something else pop into your head does it?

DJ: Yes.

LA: So would it be a good idea now that you know your brain is capable of popping something into your head when I ask you to think of something to go back and do it again so you know that your brain does pop things into your head?

DJ: Yes.

LA: OK so why don't you find yourself right now back in deep sleep. That's right just like that. And then you can sink down as deeply or lightly as you like because you know that depth is irrelevant to suggestibility. So as you find yourself in this state right here let something pop into your head *Snap!* just like that. And then because we're talking about remember to forget and forget to remember go ahead and let that happen. Let that begin to happen in the way that it may or may not have happened before because you certainly forgot to remember what it was and you remembered to

11

forget what it was. And you can do the exact same thing right now as your brain makes that happen really easily and really effortlessly.

Again, I can't tell if you're going to forget to remember what it was that popped into your head or if you're going to remember to forget first what popped into your head, if there will be a placeholder or not. But your unconscious mind can probably get to a point where no matter what it was that popped into your head you definitely will remember to forget that it was there and you'll forget to remember that it was there. And as soon as I wake you up everything about that will feel OK.

Whichever way it happens your brain will just know when it forgets to remember first or whether it remembers to forget first that you've done the exact right thing you should have done and then go ahead and come back all the way on five. One, two, three, four, and five wide awake.

DJ:   Wow. It's right there.

LA:   It's right there?

DJ:   But I can't—I know what it is but I can't say it.

LA:   That's fascinating because that's another way to do amnesia and that's not this way to do amnesia, but I'm wondering if your brain is compensating for that.

DJ:   Possibly.

LA:   So here's another interesting example. When I read about memory stuff they talk about how the right part of the brain and the left part of the brain do different things. So if I asked you–hm I want to get the correct hand down–if I asked you to write it with your left hand could you? Could you write with your left hand or draw with your left hand whatever it was?

DJ:   Uh…yes.

LA:   Isn't that fascinating? There's something about—with your left hand now can you tell me what you wrote? You're having a hard time describing it aren't you?

DJ:   Yes.

LA:   Because the language is from your left side of your brain and the right side of the brain controls your left hand so the language won't come out but the right side of your brain can draw or write whatever it was, writing is a little more challenging but you could have gotten the idea down. This is when people start to make up excuses or make up reasons for what it is that they've done because they try and get both sides to make up some cohesive thing and it doesn't get done. Can you show me what you wrote down?

DJ: Yeah.

LA: So that looks like S, A, P, E

DJ: Ah no that's actually an "O," and that's actually an "H"

LA: So S, H, O, E, shoe?

DJ: That's the one!

LA: That's really interesting. When I said it you recognized it, but until then you probably would have found yourself making up some other explanation for what it was.

DJ: Oh no, I know why. I'm comfortable enough that it's an interestingly frustrating fun experience, but I don't think I'm making an excuse for why I couldn't do it.

LA: OK so what if I told you now that you can absolutely completely remember what it was you were thinking about?

DJ: A shoe.

LA: There we go. So I have to say I'm a little surprised because I don't think I've ever used that particular phrase so many times in that particular way before, and as I know that phrasing and language has a lot to do with that sort of thing and as I was saying it I kind of felt more like it was almost a confusion induction and yet it wasn't an induction at all it was just a suggestion. I think that one will be interesting once it is written out because it might be a great induction, too.

DJ: Interesting because literally it was that I could see the concept in my mind and couldn't get it from there out.

LA: Yeah I bet we'll have a lot more interesting things like that that go on. I was in the middle of a trance one time and I was having someone forget his name, but whatever I was doing wasn't quite successful for him so he came out of trance but he was in the middle of the suggestion as he was doing it and guess who forgot his name, I remember it now but it was very weird. So ricochet can sometimes happen the other way.

DJ: Interesting, and that is interesting, wow. What's interesting is that one of the things I've always had a hard time doing is imagining things in certain contexts. For example, someone once, as the first part of a personality game, asked me, "Imagine a door. OK, what color is it?" and I'd respond, "Well, you haven't told me, what kind of door is it."

I've got the concept 'door' in my head, but I have absolutely no description whatsoever because–and I don't know if it was my legal training or not– because I had become so focused that I needed more information.

LA: So the concept was there, the details were not there?

DJ: Right. So when you say "Pop into your head" there's a slight echo of that from way back when because it's oddly frustrating to be in a position where it's throttled by that part of my brain but can certainly emphasize that for the sake of being more analytical. So I wonder if that's part of it— the thing I was told not that I have a hard time remembering...? That word. That I'm still having a hard time saying even though you said it was OK to remember it.

LA: You can remember it completely and fully and say it anytime you want right now from now on.

DJ: Shoe! There we go! It popped back into my head. You were telling me to forget to remember it and my brain was reacting like " look, I finally imagined a shoe, color, texture and everything, and I don't want to let go of that" and so it was there, in my mind's eye, but I couldn't communicate it out loud.

LA: Yeah and I think part of it is a little fascinating because some people have like what if you had someone forget a part of them that was holding them back from doing something—like what if you had someone forget they were inhibited, or that they were shy, or what if you had someone forget that they didn't know how to be funny, and then you asked them to be that way, I mean not be that way, but you asked them to be you know would they really be uninhibited, would they really be funny, would they really be bold? I mean, those are fascinating things that you could do with somebody I think to put them in a whole new state. And again is this a way they want to be forever or do you want to just give them the option that they can when they need to remember to be shy or inhibited or whatever because it serves them well because it could be.

So I guess it's that whole length of forgetting or maybe it's just installing new choices, maybe it's not really forgetting, but maybe it's good to know

14

you can forget to be a certain way sometimes. So maybe I'll have to adjust my scale. Like starting out with a scale of mild suggestions to sledgehammer suggestions may get adjusted.

DJ: Well I imagine some of it is just some things work better given the person. There's probably a reason stage hypnotists start with a lot of the times "You forget what the name of this object is" like this chair and you have to describe what the object is or you can't use the word "the" in any sentence. Those sorts of things…

LA: Oh let me share this with you. So there was somebody that I used to play with that I gave him the suggestion that for the next 24 hours they were not going to know the letter e. That there was absolutely going to be no remembering it, no use of it. They would speak normally but every time they wrote that letter would be unavailable to them, and they were a writer. Fortunately their partner did the typing when they were doing it, but for 24 hours and I was talking to them in hour 23 and 24 because they were writing everything properly except the "e." So that's a fascinating thing of what the brain can forget even though it didn't actually forget it, maybe it just remembered to not do something. I'm not sure exactly, but I think it's kind of interesting that we can do that sort of thing.

DJ: And this is becoming one long confusion induction for me.

I'm curious to why it was better for you to have me choose what to forget as opposed to suggesting something.

LA: Well because I wanted it to be something that was yours I guess. I think what I said before was that I didn't want your conscious self to fixate on it, but we could do it that way too. So what if I had you think of a straw hat and you can think of that now. And then I say deep sleep *Snap!* and then I say I know I told you something ahead of time but I want you to remember to forget what I told you and then I'd like you to forget to remember that I told you anything at all before we went in here.

So you know that you asked me for something and otherwise you absolutely remember to forget what I told you, the thing that I gave you, since we're doing this as another example and then you can forget to remember at all even that you asked for it, and maybe that would be the very best way for your brain to go about handling making sure amnesia happens in this way. That you've forgotten to remember that I told you anything and you remember to forget that I told you anything after you asked me to give you something to think about. So let's do that and then come back on five feeling great. One, two, three, four, five wide awake.

DJ:   OK… Something just happened.

LA:   OK. What just happened?

DJ:   OK… That's weird. So… I want to ask you to give me something to forget but I'm sure we've been through this before.

LA:   Are you?

DJ:   And there's something in the back of my mind that's going "Nope not here, don't look over here, nope, nope."

LA:   And you have no idea what that is.

DJ:   I have an idea.

LA:   Do you?

DJ:   But I don't want to.

LA:   Oh you have an idea but you don't want to have an idea.

DJ:   Yes.

LA:   OK so this is one of those things that make hypnotists go all happy because I know that you know that there are people that we both know that would take great delight in poking at this sort of thing and I am not above that either. However what if I told you right now that you can absolutely remember what it was right now and you can say it, you can think it, you can.

DJ:   A straw hat!

LA:   So we did in fact go through all of that before.

DJ:   Yes, we did.

LA:   See you're glaring at me like it's my fault. I mean, I will take responsibility for it but—

DJ:   No, I asked for it, I totally asked for it. No, it's brilliant. There was an unsettling thing and part of it was 'how much of this am I not supposed to remember?' Was it the whole conversation, was it the thing itself, and there was a little bit of 'I know there's a gap here,' and at the edges my mind is kind of going "Instructions were not to remember the thing and to remove it that I even asked you for something." But that part was slightly unclear, so I'm wondering when we get to the rewind is going to be really easy for me because there's a definitive "Boom."

And maybe my brain will be more amenable to sledgehammer-y type things, because I think and this might be because I'm a lawyer and there's a part of me that's like "Did she mean I wasn't supposed to remember *that* part of it or I'm not supposed to remember *that* part of it—in which case I can remember this part of it?"

LA: So which part of it could you remember if your brain said you could remember this part of it?

DJ: Well it was kind of a slow march in on it.

So, my mind was thinking, "She told me"–and even now my memory is kind of fading–"She told me not to remember the straw hat and not to remember asking for it." So the question is does that mean that whole conversation is now gone or am I supposed to remember that we led up to it, that I was going to suggest that there could be something solid that I could not remember as opposed to me coming up with something? Because that was right before that, but that implies that I may have asked about something, and what is this weird shape here that's now gone?

And so I was sort of inching my way in there at the same time that I was like "No I don't want to do that, no, stop, this is fun, I don't want to go there. I want to not remember because this is interesting and cool, so what are you doing (trying to figure it out what you were told to forget)?"

LA: Do you think that you would have remembered eventually, that it would have just popped into your head, that the part that was the barrier one day would have eventually slid away and you would have been like "Damn it, it was a straw hat" or that you just would have let it go?

DJ: I don't–interesting question–I don't know in the moment essentially, because the task is more **"C**an you remember it?" than "I'm going to be trying to remember it." But if it is in a context where I'm coming up and I'm unsettled, that's not my first question. I wonder if I would just let it go because my brain is not working against itself. Like I said there's a part of me going "Oh no, nothing here."

LA: So I think you and I both want hypnotic amnesia to work. We're not actually going "No, no, no." There are people who do that with all sorts of aspects of hypnosis because they're, I don't know, they want to have that control wrested from them like it's magic and that's not precisely the way it works. So you have to be willing on some level. I mean, there are people for whom that will work but there are people for whom that is less likely to work because they're very conscious of what it is that they won't do, and they just know that there are parts of them that will forbid that from happening, and they may need it as a safety mechanism.

I work with people who have all sorts of aversions to doing something–even if it's kind of a mild thing–especially if it has to do with giving them more pleasure. I have some people that are really like "I really don't get how to do that." But they know how to have pleasure; we're wired that way. So unless your wiring is broken or damaged (and even then we could probably find a way to rewire that), there's a part of you that's holding back. So I make these bargains with people's parts all the time.

Is there a part of you that is holding back? Yes. So is that part of you that is holding back willing to go along with everybody else for the next ten minutes? Yes. Will you let that happen starting now? Yes. OK great, do it. And then it's usually 'if this works for you will you agree in the future that you don't need to have that gate there, you can just let that happen?' And usually once they've experienced it, they're like "Yeah, this is pretty good, I'm going to go along with that," whether it's going into hypnosis, whether it's having more pleasure, whether it's forgetting something.

DJ:   Yeah, and I think I need to enlist the competitive part of me not to get into the frame of mind that is "OK, well, let's see how I can get around this," but instead enlist it into seeing "How amnesiac I can be." Because I think that part of me is approaching it as "Let's see if I can get around this." No, no. "Let's see if I can push this in a direction that does actually lead to hypnotic amnesia."

LA:   It's sort of a fascinating process to think about what it is that we can or can't do. Like we forget things all the time. I mean, it's impossible to remember everything that you do—our brains take in so much information. Our brains and our bodies, our senses take in so much information our conscious self cannot handle. We're always deleting stuff. So it's silly to think that we have a complete understanding of what's going on around us at any given time. Our eyes only see so much we've got these blind spots. Our ears only hear so much of a spectrum of sound. We're only tolerant of so many degrees of temperature before it's overload for us. We live in this really narrow, structured world, and so our conscious self is only really good at certain things within those parameters, and so I don't think it's all that unusual that we have the capacity for forgetting, or for remembering certain things. You know, it's just how we have our mind programmed, I guess.

DJ:    Now when you said that there are hypnotists, and that you were one of them, that would love to poke at this, what specifically were you referring to?

LA:    Oh, well I could see, for example, if I hadn't actually given that back to you–either the shoe or the straw hat–I could imagine because you couldn't say it and I could say the word and you could look at it and I might say, "Come on, it's really simple, I know you can do it," and I could use that as another induction. I might use that to get another response, like every time you want to say it but you can't say it, something else happens. I don't know what I would have done, but sometimes hypnotists are a little bit mischievous.

DJ:    I'm startled by the revelation.

LA:    And so having that as a fun middle point could be entertaining.

DJ:    And I want to focus on that because using these tools and techniques going forward as a way into something else is very interesting to talk about because it seems to me sometimes that can lead to a confusion induction of some sort. You're essentially overloading the brain and then dropping them farther.

LA:    And again I can't tell you exactly what I said the first time but when it gets transcribed I will look at it and I will probably find that it's a very amusing thing to put into an audio sometime and then see how well people do with remembering or forgetting something. And so this is a thought that you forgot but partly it's fun to make people forget actions. I love–and I told Chewtoy [a friend of Lee's.] about it so he wrote a story about this– but I love making people (while they're in trance) make a picture of themselves holding a sign that says "I am deeply entranced" and making them e-mail it to themselves. So eventually they get this thing that is a picture of themselves deeply in trance, and they don't remember, and I love that.

I don't care what you look like when you're in trance but you might want to know. And isn't it kind of fun to be able to know that you moved around, you walked to the point that your unconscious mind took care of you to the point that you're writing on a piece of paper walking around your house, taking a picture, sending an e-mail? Those are all fairly complex tasks… I don't know how well we get robots to do those things nowadays, but they're all fairly complex tasks, and yet there you were unconsciously, totally unaware, doing all of that and then seeing the results. And I think it's hot.

DJ: I definitely see the appeal in that. As a fellow reaction junkie I totally get that.

LA: So I think as we go further on and do more and more of these things we'll have these interesting side tangents that may or may not be relevant. But hopefully they sort of wrap up rounding out the experiences people can have and making the end result really compelling to read, and to try these things out with, and to do. I think we should put transcripts of the things that I say, not that what I say is the thing that needs to be said, it's just that it's a starting point for somebody to go "I can take this and run with this" or "I already do take this and run with this" and how much more fun can you have when you do that?

DJ: Right. I look forward to writing up my reactions to this today because I think that's going to be part of this as well.

### *Notes*

DJ: These notes were written immediately after the trance above.

*In trance, when I was instructed to forget the first item "shoe" that had popped into my head, the issue with turning it into a block on the word was personal; my wife had once had me think of a door. Then she asked me to describe the door. I couldn't actually describe the nature of the door (color, shape, component, etc.). We had had many conversations about this issue and concluded, in part, that I had spent so much time honing my analytical skills that my creative skills were left to fallow.*

*So when I was asked to pick an object, and then to forget the object, my mind actively didn't want to let go of the object. Nevertheless, it did want to comply with the request. Instead it made sure I couldn't actually say the word or answer the question. It was like I could see the image of a generic "shoe" in my mind, but wouldn't let myself answer the question.*

*I felt actual relief when I was asked to write "shoe" with my left hand. Although still frustrated that I couldn't say it yet.*

*In the second trance with "straw hat," initially I was stunned because there was a palpable gap in my head. I could feel the internal struggle between the analytical part of me that wanted to challenge the 'Amnesia' and the part of me that was cooperating in helping it happen. The analytical part of me was parsing the instructions. "So I'm not supposed to remember asking her to give me something to forget, but that means I can remember the conversation which led to that request, and it's therefore implied that I DID ask her, so I can suspect that. And if I suspect that, I can suspect that there's something I'm not remembering, and, hey! What's that weird-shaped hole in my memory right there?"*

*Meanwhile the cooperative part of my mind was wandering around, hiding the "straw hat" as if saying "Nope, nothing to see here."*

*It was a relief to remember the object, though. And it was stunning to be sitting there, coming out of that second trance, and know that there was a gap. It made my brain positively buzz.*

# CHAPTER TWO

## *Experiment 2 Let Unconscious Hide Information*

***A good place to start***
***Double binds of forgetting***
***Basic, not simple.***

The focus of the second experiment, "Let Your Unconscious Mind Hide Information from You (for some period of time)" may seem almost too simple and obvious. After all, isn't this what any of these methods are supposed to do—have the unconscious mind 'hide' things from the conscious? In the 'meta' sense, yes, that is what each of these methods does. However, in our experience, the phrase "Let your unconscious mind hide [thing] from you" is incredibly effective. Certainly more effective than just telling the subject "Forget [thing] now."

Moreover, this is the first of several experiments where the subject's unconscious is being enlisted to 'gang up' on the subject. Too often, in our experience, hypnotists neglect specifically talking directly to the unconscious. While it is true that the unconscious is part of the total person, we've found (as several future experiments make clear) that specifically talking to the unconscious and encouraging it in the endeavor increases both the efficiency and effectiveness of the methods.

In this excerpt from the second day of the overall experiment, Lee used this method to have DJ forget two items that she showed him on the computer camera. What's interesting here is that DJ's unconscious was, essentially, at war with itself, and was trying to figure out ways around the amnesiac request.

When dealing with people who describe themselves as 'control-freaks' or with people who are very competitive, be warned that they will often try to show that they're more clever than their hypnotist. They will, in fact, often look for loopholes in instructions. We'll be looking at ways of dealing with such people as we go along.

LA:   So let's turn to item number two: "Letting your unconscious mind hide information for you for this amount of time." So it could be as short as something like a game, like that Pop Quiz game [For more details, read Mark Wiseman's *Mind Play* book.] where information is right there–and usually this is what people say–"It's there, I can see it, it's right on the tip of my tongue" and they cannot get it out.

Or you can have that suggested to you, or suggest that type of thing that will happen anyway, but if you just suggest, or if I just suggest that your mind is going to know that that information is there in it, and every time your conscious self goes looking for it, you're going to move it a little further out of reach, it would be interesting to know what people's actual responses are to that. So shall we do some of that?

DJ:   Sure.

LA:   We can play that game. We can do a few other things, too.

DJ:   I'm already going into trance.

LA:   Are you?

DJ:   Yeah.

LA:   You're so easy, has anyone ever told you that? You know it's OK to be discriminating. I think you're also blushing more than I have ever seen, at this moment. It's not a bad thing to go into trance you know.

DJ:   Thank you very much. I am discriminating about whom I go into trance for... Damn it!

LA:   *Snap!* And as you think about that "Damn it" notice how effortlessly it sucks you down deeper. Notice how you can find yourself feeling really comfortable, getting into the most comfortable position for right now, and for later so that when you wake up, you wake up feeling really good.

And in the meantime think about what that's like, you've probably been in that place before, where it's felt like your unconscious mind is hiding information. No matter your age, it's not really an age thing, there was just something you were supposed to do, something you were supposed to remember and at some point in time you were like "Oh! I forgot."

And so your unconscious mind already knows how to do that and we certainly want that to happen only when it's deliberately appropriate from now on, then you really want to have those answers right there. But for right now, in this moment in time, and if I suggest it and we're still on good terms you'll notice that if I suggest your unconscious mind is going to hide some information, for a specific amount of time–whether it's an amount of time or until an event takes place–you'll find that your unconscious mind does that really easily.

And again you may find that you know an answer and it's right there, you can see it, you can hear it, you can touch it, almost. Almost on all of those things, and yet you can't quite get it out.

But the instant I tell you the answer to something or the instant I tell you that you can remember it, it's right there. The instant I tell you, it's right there.

So while your unconscious mind holds onto that thought, and as it thinks about the best way to make that happen, as it agrees to do that, just notice that your right hand can go up and touch your forehead and fall back down as your unconscious mind goes "Yes, I know how to do it; Yes, I know how to make it happen." [Pynchon's hand touches his forehead.]

Thank you. And then come all the way back up. One, two, three, four, five wide awake. Hi, so why are you smiling?

DJ:   I'm having so much fun.

LA:   All right then! So, I didn't really specify this, but I want you to consciously know what I'm going to be doing. I'm going to ask you some questions, and your unconscious mind is just going to–for the next five minutes or so– just not allow you to know what the answers to those things are.

DJ:   OK.

LA:   All right. Do you know what this is?

[Lee is holding a single jelly bean, some of which she has been eating in the build-up to this session.]

DJ:   I think I can see the word in my mind, sort of.

LA:   So you can see the thing, you can see the word sort of.

DJ:   It's two words. One of them is something you would spread on bread, and the other is something you would plant that would turn into something else.

24

LA:   And if I start singing something like "Billie Jean is not my lover…"

DJ:   If you were to sing that, yes.

LA:   Would that help your brain?

DJ:   I think it would actually make it a little worse.

LA:   Interesting. I'm eating some. Are those the words you were looking for?

[Now Lee is pointing directly at the words "JELLY BEANS" on the side of the bag.]

DJ:   Yes.

LA:   Can you say it?

DJ:   No.

LA:   Excellent. So, for the sake of our transcript, I held up a jelly bean, I showed you the bag that said "Jelly Beans."

DJ:   Yes.

LA:   And now you can say it, too.

DJ:   Jelly beans. That's going to be really difficult for me, because I'm the guy who has all the answers.

LA:   Well, that's why I said I want to make sure for trivia you still have all the answers. And in fact, somewhere in the middle of this we're going to do that thing with you, the 'increase your memory' thing with you.

DJ:   OK.

LA:   Because, you know, that way you'll have a little edge for trivia, because if you have all the answers, all you have to do is spit them out.

DJ:   That's right.

LA:   Do you always have all the answers?

DJ:   No, I don't always have all the answers.

LA:   But you often have all the answers.

DJ: Yes, my brain is like a... people say my brain is like a sponge. If you sit me down with information I can bring it in very quickly, parse it out, and recall it pretty well. I used to read almanacs cover to cover. I was a sad child.

LA: Anyway... so what else could your mind hide from you right now? It can hide your name from you.

DJ: Yes I suppose it could.

LA: Is it doing that?

DJ: Yes, it's giving me an out though.

LA: What's that?

DJ: Well I can go to a dance club and talk to the "Deejay" there.

LA: Well yeah, I didn't ask you to hide the word. So what if I ask you to hide the word for these things?

[Here, Lee holds up a pair of glasses.]

DJ: There are so many different words for those, though.

LA: Is it hiding all of them?

DJ: No, because I just went to "spectacles."

LA: What if it hid **all** the words for this? Any or all permutations of this, just not there?

DJ: [Struggles to form words.]... Yes.

LA: OK. Have it all back.

DJ: So strange, it's wonderful.

LA: So one of the things is, people might hear or read this and go "What the hell is the point of that?" right? Other than having fun with somebody else, which is still a valid reason to do it, I mean, we were talking about mind-fucks before, and that could definitely fall into that category depending on what activities were involved with that. So if somebody says, "Hey go up and tell the waiter that you need to change your order to something else." and you can't, well then you're involving a waiter in your scene, but what if it's, you know, you're at a friend's party and your friend is perfectly OK being involved in whatever it is you're doing. And that person goes up and goes "I'd like a…thing." So it can be entertaining in that kind of way. So what else could go on there?

DJ: I imagine it being–and I think we mentioned this before–it could also be the foundation for another induction, because in that moment I felt particularly confused and frankly a little vulnerable. And I can see sort of using that in the moment of confusion, you could push and maybe go into a trance, and I'm sure it would be a deeper trance because my defense mechanisms aren't up because they're more concerned about where the hell that word is.

LA: So what if the word for all these goes away right now and then you think about that really hard and then I say go down as deeply as you can right now as you are confused, and by the time you wake up, all those things can come back to you again, but you'll notice how easy it is. Indeed it was very simple for you to just go into a trance.

So on that level it works out very well. It works out very well to confuse people more and more and more. Now some people get a confused look, some people do something else.

But think about how good it feels right there, to know that, as good as your brain can be at forgetting something, it can be that much better at remembering things when the time is right, which is not during these talks about amnesia, necessarily. So go on and come all the way back right now. *Snap!*

### Notes

DJ: This one was very interesting. I could 'see' the word "jelly bean" in my brain. I could see it in front of me when Lee showed me the package, or the jelly bean itself. However, I could not bring myself to form the words either in my brain or vocally. It was like something descended in between my brain and my ability to speak. It was a struggle and it was very much a relief when she gave me back my ability to say it.

When she told me to forget my name, it was interesting that my brain went straight to the alternative meaning for the word. Likewise, when she told me to forget the word for her glasses, I went immediately to "spectacles." It was only when she had me forget ALL the words for the glasses she was holding, was I unable to formulate the words at all. (Note, when I said the word "Deejay" it, very strangely, did not sound like it was my name when I said it.)

I do wonder if it would be valuable to include an instruction that "Your mind is OK with this while we do this," because it did feel internally like I was scurrying to try to find the information. I'm also curious how people with less analytically trained minds react to these instructions.

# CHAPTER THREE

## *Experiment 3 Mail it Away*

***Mail me all your thoughts;***
***You don't need them anymore.***
***I will give them back.***

Sometimes the very act of imagining the physical activity of something can have profound internal effects. This is especially true for people who are more kinesthetic in their learning abilities, which is to say, people who respond well to suggestions of movement or motion. There are, for example several methods of hypnotic induction that rely primarily on moving, or moving with, the subject. This is, of course, difficult to do over the internet.

Nevertheless, for such people who are more kinesthetically focused, couching triggers, imagery, or instructions in terms of motion and movement can have a greater effect than other means. This can be as simple as using words that elicit feelings throughout the body ("You feel your breathing begin to slow, as you imagine yourself on the beach, feeling the wind move through your body, relaxing you.") to the amnesia instruction in this experiment.

Here, the subject is asked to imagine taking a piece of information and writing it on a slip of paper, placing that paper in an envelope, and 'sending' it to the hypnotist, thus forgetting it. To be sure, for people who are comfortable moving while under trance, the subject can actually physically do these things, up to and including actually placing the envelope in the mail, if both parties are comfortable with that. However, just the act of 'imagining' can reinforce the amnesia for kinesthetically-minded people.

Here, DJ was asked to imagine placing his address on a piece of paper. Let's see how that went.

LA:   So! Sending information out of your head to me, so DJ, deep sleep!

That's right, just go ahead and drop and sink down so effortlessly, so deeply until you find yourself in that space where you can continue to go down and down and down and down, more into trance and yet your unconscious mind is in that perfect place to take my words and make them your reality.

So no matter how deeply you go, your unconscious mind can always be in that right place, and I'd like you to think of something, think of something right now. It's going to need to be something that's meaningful to you and as you think of that something that is meaningful to you right now I'd like you to stay deeply entranced to lift your head up to open your eyes and to simply send me a little note about that thing that is meaningful to you.

You can type it, you can say it, either one is just fine, and as soon as you're done find yourself going back into that deep, deep, state of trance. Closing your eyes and letting go. Then think about every single place in your brain where that particular information is stored. Is it stored in an image somewhere or even multiple images of what the house looks like? During different seasons? Is it stored on legal documents? Is it stored on a check; other places?

Let your unconscious mind take every single place where memories about that are stored and begin to pull them in the form of ink into a pen that's in your mind. And as soon as that information has been pulled into that pen it's no longer any place in your brain except in the pen, but your unconscious is going to write that down on a piece of paper using all that information that's been pulled out of your brain and put into that pen.

[At this point, Pynchon reached over, grabbed a pen, and began scribbling on a piece of paper. He is writing down his home address on it.]

It's going to use every single last drop of that information to write that down on a piece of paper until the pen is exhausted of ink without looking without knowing because it's no longer in your brain it no longer holds any value for you, you're going to fold that up, you're going to stick it in an envelope, you're going to seal it up, you're going to turn it over, and with a different pen–a regular pen–you're going to write my name on it. Send it out of your mind. And as soon as your unconscious mind has done that find yourself waking up, wide awake. So you can see what you wrote down.

DJ:   Mmhm. [Shows the paper to LeeAllure.]

LA:   What is that?

DJ:   Like… what I wrote to you?

LA:   Yes.

DJ:   Like what my actual… fuck. [Pynchon is staring at the sheet of paper.] I've got a bunch of numbers and I've got a street name.

LA:   Yeah.

DJ:   Nice, I've got nothing.

LA:   What's nice?

DJ:   I can't remember it.

LA:   Any of it? Did the numbers go when you thought about them or what?

DJ:   It's like I can't get there. It's like they're a jumble, it's like I occasionally get glimpses of it but I couldn't tell you what they are. And there's a back door way I can get to the street name because of something else, but it'd be like running through molasses to get there.

LA:   Yes, that might be a little sticky.

DJ:   Yes, very much so.

LA:   Alright, so have it all back now.

DJ:   Wow—darn.

LA:   So you wrote down your home address.

DJ:   Yes, I went through a few things before I decided to try to forget the address.

LA:   Yeah, let's hear them.

DJ:   You said to choose something meaningful, and because of conversations we've been having about someone who was asked to choose something in the past that they could change like the worst thing possible. It was like I went through, I don't want to forget that I'm married, or my dog's name.

LA:   Well you know the point of these is not necessarily for you to go "Oh, I forgot that I was married, I forgot that I had a dog." It's just to show that your mind can withhold information from you if it's directed to, if it chooses to, if something seems more important.

DJ: And part of it is I wanted to do this for the experiment because I wanted to do it. I didn't want to make it more complicated than it needed to be, so I figured choosing something that was my home address, easy-peasy. It's not the end of the world if I forget my home address.

LA: You could learn it again if you had to. I said you could learn it again if you had to.

DJ: Exactly, but that was cool. That was really interesting. It was very much like the number, I briefly saw the number and then it was gone in like a jumble every time I tried to think of it. The street name I just couldn't accept that, except that I knew it was one letter off from a famous city and I could see the city and any time I tried to work back to the street name I couldn't do that. It was like "No, no I know it's right there, but no."

LA: You know it's funny because I talk a lot about un-limiting yourself, and I'm not saying that forgetting is a skill necessarily, and yet it kind of is. And some people are reluctant to acquire a skill because they're afraid it means they don't have the other. And so the converse of this would be to have an excellent memory.

DJ: Right.

LA: But I think that when your brain understands that it can hold onto or let go of information based on something that you prioritize for it, or is prioritized for it based in a certain specific instance with certain specific standards around it, then your brain can learn what's important to you and go 'oh well, these are things I'm going to hold onto, these are things I'm going to always know, these are things that are just going to be useful for me.'

And I don't mean always know, like, I'm going to get this tattoo and it's going to look awesome when I'm 90. I actually did see a thing on tattoos with senior citizens, and they looked pretty cool. But it's not like they showed a tattoo close up, a lot of them had —their bodies were canvases let's just say. So is there some information that's tattooed onto our mind that maybe will distort and twist over time and yet could always be there? I think the answer might be yes, although maybe tattooing isn't the best because it's not always in the same place. And again we remember and we can get to memories in all sorts of ways. Whether it's "I can see it on a map," or whether "It's just like this other city but not quite," you know. There are fascinating ways in which our minds work and who knows what might trigger this flood of information? I don't know. Except I do know that saying you can have that back worked pretty well.

DJ: It works fantastically well and it's such a relief, because internally, once you remove it, part of my brain is like, "I want that back, where is it?" and it is scampering around trying to figure out ways to get to it.

LA: I wonder if we added in "And you feel completely comfortable with the knowledge that you don't have that information," I wonder what that would do?

DJ: And/or, you know this will come back to you in an area of time depending on what area we're trying to work at.

LA: Well your information can certainly be returned to you at a time. I don't know why, Tuesday at seven o'clock is always my favorite time. I'm not sure why that is. So to let your brain just get to the place where that's what it does is pretty cool.

## Notes

DJ: This was strangely effective. I could briefly see the numbers of my address, and I'm sure that if I had really needed them, I could access them. Or, at least, that's what I told myself. I pictured in my mind's eye the action of writing the address down. I was vaguely surprised that I was actually doing it; it felt a little like I was doing the action in a dream. I'm not the most kinesthetic of people (some have accused me of living in my own brain) but the physical act of writing the address down while being told that the act was 'sucking' the information out of my brain, if you will, was a whole different experience.

For the life of me I couldn't grasp those numbers or the street name as I stared at them. Looking back on it, it seems crazy that I didn't recognize my own address, but I still remember that cool, unsettling, feeling like it was yesterday.

(I was gratified that my mind settled on something that was 'important' but not 'necessary' or something that had emotional currency.)

Again, the relief when I was allowed to access the information was palpable. It was like a block had been removed and a muscle I had was allowed to work again.

# CHAPTER FOUR

## *Experiment 4 Restricted Access Room*

***Inaccessible***
***Yet tucked within your own mind;***
***Trust me with the key.***

Putting information in a room only the hypnotist and the unconscious can access.

This experiment expands on the premise of the previous experiment. However, where that one was based on the concept of sending information out of the subject's head via a hypothetical (or real) letter, this one involves taking the information and hiding it deep within the subject's own brain. Here, the hypnotist asks the subject to create a room that only the hypnotist and the unconscious can access, deep within the mind. The hypnotist then places some information within that room.

This has similar purposes to the previous experiment, inasmuch as it, in part, relies on vaguely kinesthetic modalities for its effectiveness. That said, this version is probably better suited for more creative types, or people who are usually "in their heads."

As DJ will remark at the end of the chapter, this method was profoundly effective on him (possibly because he considers himself very much "in his own head"). Because it comes up in the conversation, and is relevant, it should also be noted that he had recently hit his thumb while hammering a nail shortly before this session was recorded.

LA:  So I think this information, the fourth one–put information deep inside a room only your unconscious mind and I can reach–must be something that you don't know what it is ahead of time.

DJ:  OK.

LA: So I'm going to write a few things down, and I'm going to just write a few phrases and we'll see which ones your unconscious mind holds onto, one or all of them.

Well, I'm thinking what's the best way to put you into a trance right now?

But I think you already know the answer to that, and you can just make it happen. Yup, just like that, really effortlessly down. Sinking and dropping down, deeper, and deeper, and deeper still. And feel how very good it is to just get right there, and then to give in a little bit more. And then give in still more. Notice how good it feels to sink down deeply, deeply, deeply in trance.

As you find yourself there, let your unconscious mind send your conscious self off. Let your unconscious self go to a place wherever inside you, in that infinity, it might be that has these criteria: wherever it is your conscious self will always pass by it, completely unaware that it's there; if your conscious self ever becomes aware this place is there, that information just slides right out of your head on the conscious level. So this is a place that only your unconscious mind and I can occupy.

Whatever it is about your conscious self–the size, the shape, the smell, the sound, the feeling of it, whatever it is–it simply is unable to get in. It always remains outside, it always remains as unaware as possible, and again, if it ever becomes aware of it, it simply forgets it very quickly. Forgets why it was important, anything like that, until the information I share with your unconscious mind in there–whether it's really important information or really unimportant information–ceases to become important.

The thing that is important is that this is a room where your unconscious mind and I can share information, and that information stays locked in this room until I take it out, and your unconscious mind holds onto or perhaps the room itself holds onto the information—only letting me and your unconscious self in. If your unconscious self is OK letting that happen, knows that place that fits those requirements, and is going to take us there right now, let that happen and raise your hand up to your head and just let it drop down as you sink more deeply into trance. [DJ does so.] Thank you.

I'm going to give you three pieces of information for your unconscious self to know.

**Green dolphins live to eat fish.**

**Grassy water comes from rock wells.**

And you may already know this information but that's OK, because I'm going to tell you something personal about it. So you may know the factual thing about this on a conscious level and that's fine, but your conscious self will not know that we talked about this, and that's OK, too.

**Arkansas has the United States' only real diamond mine, and some day I'm going to go mine diamonds there.**

As soon as your unconscious mind has processed those three pieces of information, has known that they're in that room, in that space, that your conscious self is simply unaware of, and your unconscious self is good with making sure that's the way it is always going to be, then you can find yourself coming up, wide awake. Hi.

DJ:   Hi.

LA:   So what are you thinking about now?

DJ:   I went really deep.

LA:   You went really deep.

DJ:   And darn you.

LA:   Darn you for putting you into a deep trance?

DJ:   Yes… no… I put myself into a deep trance?

LA:   Interesting. So do you consciously remember what I told you?

DJ:   About what?

LA:   While you were deeply in trance.

DJ:   Currently not. Yeah I keep on coming up to something and then going away from it.

LA:   What do you keep coming up to?

DJ:   I sort of know what it is but I can't say.

LA:   What is it that you sort of know that it is?

DJ:   I don't know!

LA:   OK.

DJ:   It's really fascinating.

LA: Well, so I told you three different things and they're not things that are important for you because there's very little fact in there. And the one thing that was factual was about me not about you, but it's kind of interesting to know that your unconscious can create a place that your conscious self cannot get into.

DJ: Right. So what's really great about this sort of place to have on a practical level, why do you want to do this?

LA: I like to do it because I like to become better friends with the unconscious self on some level. And I think it's helpful if the unconscious knows that it's completely trusted to always have the person's best interest at heart and to know that sometimes it involves holding onto information in a way their conscious self doesn't have to pay attention to. I think it's also interesting to give you triggers or commands that can fit in there, that can be activated by your unconscious alone.

DJ: What would an example of that be?

LA: Well it's not that…so, sometimes that goes on to some of the other things that I do.

For example, if I was really doing heavy conditioning with someone and I wanted them to make sure that every single day at a certain time they were doing something, but to not know about it. Like sometimes I tell people they're going to do something every day at a certain time and it's just fine. But what if I wanted someone to get into a habit and even though the unconscious mind is way more powerful than the conscious self, we can sort of sabotage what we do occasionally if we're not careful with our conscious minds.

So what if I wanted to help someone set up a really good habit for something, and we talked about it and I set it up with the unconscious mind that it was just going to begin to do these things? It doesn't necessarily have to have it's own place. Erickson used to do all sorts of hypnosis with people without that particular technique and people would often forget that they had even ever smoked or ever had the issue that they went to him for. Which is kind of a fascinating thing, so your mind already can just move on and say "I'm the kind of person who never smoked," or "Why would I smoke?" or whatever it happens to be.

DJ: Right.

LA:    But I liked the idea that you could actually take that and give someone a new habit really easily without them being aware of it until all of a sudden it just became part of who they were. Is that always super useful? I can, I'm pretty sure that you can, twist things around to the not good, but I think it can be used for all kinds of good too, like if someone is having an issue with something and it would be better if they just made whatever– something else happen–you can do that. And all of a sudden they're behaving a little better than they were. I'm not saying it's like you make someone go from being a slob to being the most clean person around but just little incremental things and all of a sudden someone's doing something differently.

DJ:    And how does this method–I'm having a hard time forming the words it's because of the trance–how does this method help that?

LA:    So if I put information deep inside a room that only your unconscious mind and I can reach, and how does that help?

Because if your conscious self isn't getting in the way of you doing something or not doing something, if it's really kind of unaware and you just find yourself doing something, you may not be paying attention to that thing your unconscious mind does because we're so used to paying zero attention to the things that our unconscious mind does.

And when you know that all of a sudden you're just doing something…like what if I was going to do something very useful for you, but I'm going to talk to you about it first. So what if every next time that you had a hammer in your hand, you only ever hit the thing you were supposed to hit?

DJ:    OK, I think that sounds like a fantastic idea.

LA:    Right? So maybe on an unconscious level, or maybe on a conscious level, you're putting your hand in a weird spot and you're not being precise enough to where you hit, but what if I talked to your unconscious mind and said "By the way," deep in that room, "From now on any time DJ has a hammer in his hand you are going to make sure his muscle movements are accurate and that they always hit the thing they are supposed to hit, avoiding completely, keeping safe completely, any fingers, body parts, etc., whether they're eyes when you swing back or whatever. So you find that your movements with the hammer become much more precise.

So that's the sort of thing you can do in somebody's unconscious mind where the unconscious mind goes "Oh yeah, I guess part of us didn't like being hit with that hammer, we had big band-aids on, we were bleeding," whatever, because the unconscious doesn't always realize when it is doing something that is uncomfortable to the conscious self, because the conscious self sort of gets this super self-awareness even though it's only super aware of maybe five percent of what's going on. And the unconscious is busy running all these processes, and it's not paying attention. So there's feedback for some things but there's not feedback for a lot of things.

So you've got to able to say, "Hey, wait a minute," you've got this process deep down somewhere that says "When we swing a hammer we don't really care about it, it's not important to us." And so you can adjust that and say, "We'd like this to become important to you." so that all the body, not just the mind, can stay safe when you do this activity. Well that's the sort of thing that you can make happen.

Now we've just had this conversation while you're conscious but fractionated. However I'm telling you right now that information because your unconscious mind is paying attention to what I say can just sink and go in there and begin to make that happen.

And you can at some point in time forget that we've ever had this discussion, but the next time you go and do anything with a hammer whether it's putting a thing in a wall, or whether it's garden stuff, or anything else–you decide to build a shed, and extension onto your house, whatever–your hands are perfectly safe you don't hit yourself in the head or the shin or whatever. I think that's sort of a win-win kind of thing.

DJ:   It is, I've never hit myself in the head with a hammer, but nevertheless I appreciate it.

LA:   I was going for the worst-case scenario, I would hope you would never hit your head with a hammer. There you go.

### Notes

DJ:   This was another strangely effective session for me. Perhaps not so strange, since I do believe I 'live inside my own head.' Prior to this, it did feel a little like I was 'playing along.' Which is often a shorthand explanation for "The subject is in a light trance and still following instructions." Here, however, despite my best efforts, I couldn't quite get at the information Lee had put in the secret room. Here's what I wrote later that day:

*This seems to be working fine. Of course, I have no conscious idea what was placed in there. (The word Arkansas comes up for some reason. And dolphin. But beyond that, nothing.) So Lee will have to describe this (or else I'll have a nice surprise if I wind up transcribing it).*

A short time ago, and roughly six months after Lee and I had this session, we did a presentation on "Hypnotic Amnesia" at a hypnosis conference in San Francisco. I pulled up the notes Lee had prepared on all our sessions for the class on a laptop and we used that as the basis for a summary of our work. For this experiment, she had written down the things I was to lock away in the room. Nevertheless, and, I repeat, six months later, I still couldn't remember those things. In fact, I looked at the words, and couldn't retain the information, nor could I read them to the class. Briefly, in front of the class, Lee gave me the ability to remember one of the lines and then, with a snap, took it away again. I was told I struggled to say the words, even with permission. I'll have to take their word for it.

To this day, as I poured over the transcript for this chapter, my mind and my eyes skipped over that portion of the transcript. And, as far as I know, Lee has done no reinforcement of this method.

So yes, for me, this is a very powerful method.

# CHAPTER FIVE

## *Experiment 5 Sudden Wake Up*

***Startled and awake***
***You can lose track of your thoughts***
***Wake! And–poof!–it's gone.***

This method requires the subject to be in a trance and then be woken up suddenly. It relies on the fact that, particularly after a sudden reawakening, the subject is often a little at sea. Often times, in fact, the subject will feel like they may have gone deeper than they actually have. Because of how it requires the subject to already be in a trance, this is a very situational method.

When the subject is thrown out of trance quickly, the conscious mind is often left scrambling and, essentially, 'forgets' what just happened. It's situational inasmuch as it's probably more effective when the subject doesn't see it coming. This, of course, makes consent a trifle tricky. You probably want some level of blanket consent for memory play before embarking on this method.

LA:  Well I'm trying to think of the best way to make this happen. So you know that's the other thing—if I'm planning for success and the instructions are "Wake them up suddenly" and the implication is "And cause amnesia with whatever you told them to do while in that trance state," are there other things…

I mean, do I just tell you that you're going to forget, do I just wake you up suddenly? And so this is much like "Remember to forget and forget to remember" for me because I'm having to figure out the framework that it's going to work best in. I'm really looking forward to [Experiment] number six by the way.

But it doesn't really matter anyway. DJ, deep sleep right now. Deeper, and deeper, and deeper that's right. Effortlessly sinking down so nicely in that place where your unconscious mind remembers reading what you were reading and that's all your conscious mind can focus on right now–what you were reading and what you were about to say, just hold onto those things–and then in the meantime you can… no I don't know, you can just keep going down, and down, and down some more.

Letting your unconscious be at that place where it's most suggestible, remembering what I said—the goal is to have you be in amnesia when I wake you up suddenly. So let's see how your unconscious mind can make that happen. Wake up right now.

DJ:   You just did something didn't you?

LA:   Did I?

DJ:   Yes.

LA:   I think that's called wake them up suddenly.

DJ:   I think that, too.

LA:   That's what I just did.

DJ:   I've got that yummy feeling.

LA:   See that's the hard thing, when someone gets that yummy feeling, you can take that yummy feeling away, whatever that is. I mean, I could ask your unconscious mind the next time I woke you up that way–or until I gave it back to you–to take away those feelings so you would feel exactly the way you did when you were normally wide awake.

Because the unconscious mind can make that happen too. So I didn't do that, but you can, and that gives somebody less of an idea that they were entranced. I'd say that's really fascinating because if someone has no internal notice that they've been in trance… If they don't have any internal notice, whether it's a yummy feeling, whether it's a tingling, something that they're aware of–if they don't have that, and that's their tell usually–if you've taken away their tell then how do they know they have been in trance? They don't and that's a really interesting way to use amnesia.

DJ:   Good because I remember you telling me about the person who had tingling on the scalp I guess, and that's how they knew they had just been in trance because that was the one thing they were holding onto when you were playing with amnesia with them and then you just took that away from them.

LA:   Yes, I did it for trance amnesia specifically, they just always had that when I woke them up from trance. They're a good subject too–and when I took it away they didn't know at all that they'd been in trance. I did give it back to them. Removing it was more an experiment in what could happen when it was gone.

DJ:   And what's interesting is that I'm sitting here and when you first brought me up I had the yummy feeling and I had a bit of a memory of what had happened. And the farther on that we're going, the only reason I know I was in trance is because I had a yummy feeling and I have less and less idea of what actually happened.

### Notes

DJ:   It was only when reading the transcript for this that I even remembered that we had done this. In fact, my notes from this day's session include this at the end verbatim:

*Did we do "Wake them up suddenly"*

Judging from the transcript, the only reason I thought that I had even been in a trance was because (as I state) there is usually a 'yummy feeling' I associate with a trance. I have a vague recollection that I was talking with Lee and blinked, and then there was that post-trance feeling. Everything else seems gone, except for this transcript.

# CHAPTER SIX

## *Experiment 6 Interrupt and Resume*

***You sit there, talking***
***Drop! And count down to twenty!***
***Resume; as you were.***

This method–interrupt the subject in the middle of something else, then bring them back, and continue on as if nothing happened–is very much a complement to the previous experiment, only where the subject there is interrupted in trance, more or less, here the subject is interrupted while awake.

Again, the amnesia is encouraged by the 'shock' to the system.

We struggled with this one, not so much because of the method itself, but because DJ had a hard time with the instruction that was given, as we'll see below.

Ultimately, we settled on a markedly different instruction.

LA:   Number six is going to be a lot of fun. That's the whole interrupt somebody in the middle thing.

DJ:   Right.

LA:   And again that's one of those things that you sort of want to like…

DJ:   That you want to build up to and…

LA:   Actually no, and I'm going to demonstrate that for you. I mean, right now I'm sort of in the trigger, out of trance behavior mode but that's alright. I'm really kind of keyed up because I've been running around all morning. And so I'm like… I don't feel like I'm in a yummy mode. My body is in sort of a stressed ready for flight sort of thing. I don't know what it is.

DJ: Oh OK, do you not want to do this now or…?

LA: Oh no, it's fine.

DJ: OK.

LA: It's just one of those things. I think because I had to bake today, well 'had to' is not really the right term. So basically I've moved all my stuff out of the kitchen. Except the problem is I'm actually a cook. Like I cook and I bake and I take raw ingredients and I make stuff.

DJ: Awesome.

LA: Right. And so I have all this stuff because I use them in the kitchen. And so I had to get all this stuff together but my stuff that wasn't anywhere near the kitchen and it was kind of weird and it was kind of weird to cook in a place where you didn't have stuff? Like I went camping for a long time so it wasn't like I had no kitchen, I just had a teeny tiny kitchen.

And I had a stove where you poured an ounce of alcohol in and it lit it up, it was made out of a beer can… So I had a little teeny tiny kitchen, everything works just fine in the little teeny tiny kitchen, and

Deep sleep!

That's right you can remember consciously the fact that you were scratching your chin and talking about my teeny tiny kitchen, and maybe about to ask me a question. And deeper sleep now, deep, deep, deep, deep, deep down. And when you find yourself waking up you'll find that perhaps you have a question you want to ask me, but I'm going to keep talking about that teeny tiny kitchen and you're going to go on scratching your chin as though nothing else ever happened.

And in the meantime deeper and deeper and deeper down right now. So I'm going to ask you to do something else right now. Let's go to that room, that room that only your unconscious mind and I can go to, and as we go there I'm going to give you a trigger for later, and basically it goes like this: from now on whenever you see me take a drink out of my glass, out of a tea cup, out of a water bottle, whatever, your mind probably knows what I'm going to tell it to do already, but I'm going to tell you to do it anyway. You're going to clap your hands, go "Hypnosis is awesome," and then you're going to continue going on doing whatever it is you were doing.

Much like, in fact, this particular trance as you find yourself dropping down, down, down, down right now and as your unconscious mind is going to ensure that your conscious self lets you carry on where you were, your unconscious is going to make sure that from now on you find yourself automatically with that behavior as long as it's safe and appropriate, and as long as we're still friends.

You can make that happen. And then as your unconscious mind agrees to do it, I would like you to wake up and scratch your chin at the moment that you do it.

[DJ has a hard time raising his hand to scratch his chin.]

It's OK to have a little internal struggle, I have faith in your unconscious self.

[Here, DJ raises his hand.]

Yes? Did you want to come out of trance and say something? Go back in, come back out, up.

DJ: Uh, some sort of resistance to that one, the clapping hypnosis is fun while you drink.

LA: Hmm, why is that?

DJ: I don't...the phrase, ironically, "Trained monkey" comes to mind.

LA: Oh, well, that's bizarre. Well, I certainly don't see you that way.

DJ: Can we limit it for purposes of talking online?

LA: Of course.

DJ: OK, thanks.

LA: You're welcome. So as you find yourself knowing that we can limit it for that purpose only, for just online, and as you find the resistance to that particular thing dissolving because we've changed the parameters a little bit, can your unconscious mind hold on to what we've said without your conscious self feeling that worry or any guilt or any negative things at all? In fact, can you just feel really good, and sink down deeper, and deeper?

And as you sink down deeper just let those things wash away, not the suggestions, they can stay deeply in that room for your unconscious self, but you can feel as good as you did before I made those suggestions and you needed the clarification.

And then when your unconscious mind is ready for that, you can let me know that you're OK with those things by reaching up scratching your beard and instantly waking up at that time where we were.

[DJ wakes up.]

Yeah so it was really super tiny.

DJ:  Is that the beer can…?

LA:  Yeah it basically gets folded inside itself and it's really tiny, it's only about this big and then the inside is filled with this wicking, burnable–it doesn't actually burn but wicking material that holds the alcohol so you get kind of like a ring burner–so it's pretty cool. I also have a little screen around it, a wind screen. And it's about the size of a beer can so it's not really big, but it's big enough for all the lightweight cooking pots that you might have.

[Lee takes a drink from her cup.]

DJ:  Hypnosis is fun.

LA:  And so I really like that you can make that happen. You have that look again.

DJ:  Yes I do.

LA:  Why do you have that look again?

DJ:  This rocks. You had me under at some point.

LA:  Yes and not just once but twice now.

DJ:  Twice…

LA:  Well, once for the 'wake them up suddenly' and once for the 'interrupt somebody in the middle of something and then carry on as you were.'

And so you actually have two suggestions for that second one, both that thing that you just did–what did you just do?–and the other thing which is to not remember that you were in trance.

DJ:  Cool. [DJ waves his arms wildly.] Ah so much fun.

[Lee takes a drink.]

Hypnosis is fun.

LA: So, I will tell you that you had a resistance to that.

DJ: Yeah, but I'm not surprised.

LA: Well, you said to me that the phrase "Trained monkey" came to mind.

DJ: OK.

LA: And I told you that's not how I intended it so I adjusted it, we adjusted it together so that it would be just for when we're online.

DJ: OK, I have a vague memory of that happening.

LA: Remember it now.

DJ: Now. Yes, now. Oh that's awesome.

LA: Yeah, it's fun isn't it?

DJ: It is very much fun. I can see why people want to play more with this.

LA: Right. Because when you discover that you've done something and you didn't know it was coming and you did or you did it and you go "Why the hell did I do something," and then you go "Oh I know why I did it."

DJ: Yeah, because something just happened.

LA: Right, and that's really cool.

DJ: That is really cool. Oh, I want to do more of both sides of this.

LA: Yes, you do. Yeah.

DJ: Oh wow. Yeah, and it is very much like receding into the distance now.

LA: Yeah, they just sort of fade away and it's not important really, but I will tell you this… when you go, I mean, I know we're going to have different words because we don't speak the way the other speaks, but when you go to do these things with other people you may notice that my words come out of your head the first time and then your conscious self has gone "Oh, I get that…"

DJ: Sure, I get how this works and I can totally get the power trip on the other side of it, too.

LA: Yeah it's fun. Well, I don't know and again I don't like that phrase, "Trained monkey," because it's never how I see people, and I guess if I thought that way then every suggestion would be that way. But none of the suggestions are that way. It's more like an exercise in what can you do and how adept can your unconscious mind become at doing all sorts of fascinating things.

DJ: And I think part of it for me is I like the power exchange dynamic [Lee takes a drink from her cup.]– hypnosis is fun–and where it's a bit of a struggle.

LA: Well I'm pretty sure when you do this with other people you won't feel that way about them and so to let it go because about yourself is easy, too. To know that it's less about performance per se, or that it's less about performing and more about performance, does that make sense?

DJ: No, what do you mean?

LA: I mean, it's less about putting on a show and more about demonstrating your ability to make something happen.

DJ: As a hypnotist?

LA: Yeah and also as a subject because your unconscious mind is going, "Yeah I can make this happen, it's simple for me to do it and here we go it's done."

[After a brief break.]

DJ: So the "Trained monkey" thing, I was thinking about it when we were off, and I think part of it is the submissive part of me is fine with being submissive, but it isn't going to kneel because someone says "Kneel," it sort of has to be earned.

LA: OK.

DJ: And I think having that reaction to just a drink of water when it can have absolutely nothing to do with me, there's a part of me that feels that that's too easy. Because I think there's a part, and I don't know if this is true of all submissives or whatever, but you want the service to be special for some sort of reason and so tagging that to sort of something that is just sort of innocuous.

LA: Well I'll tell you why I did it–because when I first started out I needed some way to know that the people I was hypnotizing were really hypnotized and not playing along. And for me that was the way that I knew that someone was doing that—that they were in that mindset as opposed to some other mindset. And it's been remarkably good for letting that happen, it doesn't have to be that. It could be almost anything that gives me an answer to something without the other person knowing that I've asked them a question.

DJ: Right and I think it works tremendously well, I think it works fine. I'm just saying that for my own internal dynamics I think that's why I was so resistant to it because I…it isn't a specific trigger command that has to go out of it's way to happen, it can just be a snap. I'm attuned to that sort of thing anyway so I think my mind is just sort of wrestling with that in general. But it's cool that it worked too, it's like, pretty awesome.

LA: Yeah, I don't know, I like that exercise, that demonstration that the unconscious mind can pay attention and can do almost anything. And so it could have been anything else. So maybe we can think of anything else that could have been useful.

DJ: Hmm, before we go to anything else, the other thing that still sticks in my conscious mind is for some reason is "If we're still friends," and that sort of has crept up even though I barely have any memory of anything else…

LA: Well that is because I want to make sure. You know, I can't guarantee what happens in this life so if I die, you know, or if I tie a trigger to me and all of a sudden we had some massive blowout—I'm not planning on it, but stranger things have happened. And I like to give people the opportunity to understand–and sometimes maybe I hammer this in more than I really have to–that you have the ability in your mind to know what is going on, to be proactive for yourself, and to be able to automatically not have things work, whether its me, or somebody else, if something happens.

DJ: If it's not appropriate for whatever reason, and actually this is a conversation I was having with my wife last night where her fear is "Dear god what if something gets implanted that doesn't work and your brain seizes upon it and goes in completely the wrong direction?" And I'm like "I'm pretty sure… I would not be involved in this if I was not sure I could clear out my brain of these things if for whatever reason it wasn't working for me."

And I think that does get lost in a lot of conversations about hypnosis. As much as it's a dance between the hypnotist and the person being hypnotized, the person being hypnotized does have a lot of power to just say no.

LA: And sometimes I liken it to "We're going for a drive and you're in the driver's seat but I'm telling you where to go and I'm showing you all these fabulous places that you've never been to before.". Or maybe "I'm taking you to fabulous places that you've been to before but because I'm in the car it's a slightly different ride than it's ever been."

And you can certainly take your car and put it back in its own garage, but you can't really undo the things that you've learned, but you don't have to keep doing them in the future, or you don't have to keep doing them with the same person in the future. You have this opportunity to have control over what it is you want to do and who you do it with, and what your brain is OK with. So there. And that's why I add that in.

DJ: OK excellent, then my conscious mind can sort of get rid of that particular command now, although it'll be fun at a later date I'm sure. Awesome. I'm having so much fun. Did you want to a different thing for a trigger later or...

LA: Well I'm trying to discover one now, see what my mind comes up with that might be appropriate for you, that your brain would be like "Oh yeah I'm all over that, I'm so all over that." But I don't know what that is yet.

DJ: I feel like I should go down the trigger list at some point because there're some fun ones in there.

LA: Yeah?

DJ: Yeah. I love the pause and freeze ones, those are really fun to work with. There's some part of me that enjoyed being tickled and not being able to do anything about it.

LA: Yeah, that's good isn't it? I wonder if you can feel that again right now. Yes, you can.

DJ: Yes, I can.

[And at this point DJ loses it as he's being hypnotically tickled.]

### Notes

DJ: The first time this was done, it did seem to work, though because it was the first time we had done an actual trance, I felt the residual 'yummy' feeling I get from trance. That seemed to indicate that a trance had just occurred despite me having no specific memory of it. Interestingly, as I initially came up, I seemed to have some memory of the trance itself. However, that faded away in the distance, so to speak, as time went on.

When she did the interrupt in the middle of her cooking story, I was certain, for some reason, that I had already been hypnotized and that her constant use of the word "stuff" was a trigger for something. I was more or less focused on that when she brought me under.

Later, as we'll see, she substituted in a different reaction to her taking a drink of water. We'll see those effects in Experiment Seven.

I'm glad my subconscious mind was able to 'protect' me from things that I might otherwise not be amenable to. It was actually gratifying to be able to say "No" to that suggestion, and this seemed to let me go deeper subsequently.

# CHAPTER SEVEN

## *Experiment 7 White Room*

*White, peaceful, quiet.*
*Soundproofed room keeps thoughts out.*
*Unconscious knows all.*

*Are there black curtains?*
*Or just your thoughts locked away?*
*They hide from themselves.*

This method, "Putting the information in a white room" is another variant on the soundproofed room in Experiment Four. Only here, the subject is asked to imagine a white soundproofed room. The imagery used to convey the method is meant to appeal to subjects who are more visually oriented in nature; describe what the room looks like, what might be in it, and stress that it's separated from the rest of the subject's mind.

The actual trance itself followed immediately on from Experiment 6 and, due to the mischief of Lee, led into a preview of a later Experiment, fractionation.

LA:  Let's see, DJ deep sleep. Just like that. Down, down, down, down, down, down, down so much more deeply down than ever before, letting your unconscious paying attention to my voice and let your unconscious put your conscious self in a totally separate room right now.

This room is going to be sound proofed, super comfortable, I think of it as being a white room but that's so that your conscious self can put whatever it wants there, but notice that it's peaceful.

There's so much super comfy furniture in there. Maybe there's something to watch, a TV or something, I don't know. But it's so soundproofed that even if there's a window the sound of my voice is simply unable to get through.

It's so far away and so totally soundproofed that only your unconscious mind can hear my voice and of course your unconscious mind gets a little bit greedy and holds my words and my voice all to itself.

And as your unconscious mind does that let's adjust that trigger. So from now on, when we're on camera only when you see me take a glass of water, a drink of water, no matter what you're in the middle of doing you just pause for two seconds–one 1,000, two 1,000–and you just carry on with whatever it was you were doing.

And I bet your unconscious mind can find itself finding that more fun, and as your unconscious mind agrees to do that, finding it more fun, just go ahead, reach up, scratch your beard and wake up instantly.

[DJ reaches up and scratches his beard, waking up.]

DJ:   Um…

LA:   Yes?

DJ:   So much fun.

LA:   It is, I know.

DJ:   Wow. I was under again?

LA:   Yes that was number seven.

DJ:   Seven?

LA:   Mmhm, that was 'put your conscious self in a separated room, soundproof and white.'

     [Throughout, Lee is taking sips of water and DJ is pausing for two-second intervals.]

DJ:   Seven times under?

LA:   No that was three times under.

DJ:   OK, well, I lost track. If you had told me seven that would have been a mind fuck.

LA:   Would it? Yeah. Deep sleep.

Down deeper, and deeper, and deeper.

You can in fact forget that you woke up and that would be OK too. But tell you what, because seven would be a mind fuck I bet eight would be a mind fuck, too.

So what I'm going to ask you to do—and I'll ask your unconscious mind when I'm done, when it's accepted this—to begin to make it happen, touch your beard again. You'll find yourself instantly awake, but when you realize you're instantly awake, then go back down for number five.

Then come up and scratch your beard for number six or come down for number six. Just give yourself a few seconds. You might even begin talking. You might even remember consciously that you're doing that until you've done that cycle, until you've been in trance five more times.

So begin that now, thank you.

DJ:   Um, so uh…

[DJ drops down again. Reaches up and scratches his beard.]

LA:   Nicely done.

DJ:   And it's a really…

[DJ drops down *again*. Reaches up and scratches his beard. He seems unable to speak.]

LA:   Number six. And yes, really. That's right, just like that.

[DJ drops down yet again. Reaches up and scratches his beard.]

LA:   That's seven, and I bet you're going to be very nicely fractionated, before you go down and then come up again for good. Well, until you go down again of course.

[The cycle repeats one more time.]

LA:   And that's eight. Do you remember? Will you remember, will you forget, I don't know. Whatever it is best for you to have a good time with, that's what you'll do.

DJ:   [Collects himself.] Holy crap Batman!

LA:   Yes. So what were you saying?

DJ:    I don't remember.

### *Notes*

DJ:    By the end of this day's session (which encompassed Experiments 5, 6 and 7) I was very, very fractionated. To be honest, reading through the transcript was probably the first time I remembered much of this happening. My notes for the day actually, upon review, confused my reactions to Experiments 6 and 7.

Here are the notes I was able to salvage from this portion:

*The fact that a trigger was given and it worked was such a wonderful experience. It was that brief moment of surprise you remember when magic tricks were new. I can see why that sense of wonder can be addicting, or, at least, something you'd want to get back to over and over again.*

*So... not very helpful. I can say that, even now, when Lee and I are on a video-chat meeting I still do pause every time she takes a drink from a cup, but until I read this transcript I could not have told you when it started.*

# CHAPTER EIGHT

## *Experiment 8 Focus on Something Else*

**Distraction does work**
**Consume your attention right there**
**Things slide right by you.**

The method of having the conscious mind think of something else essentially uses a method of distraction for the conscious mind. By focusing the 'conscious' mind on some other thing, the unconscious mind will absorb whatever information is sent to it, without the subject 'remembering.'

It's probably a good idea to have the conscious mind focus on something pleasant and/or something that the conscious mind can be absorbed by, so to speak.

In this case, Lee had DJ focus on a particular soccer team he is a fan of. (We've changed the reference to protect Mr. Pynchon's identity.)

LA:   All right, deep sleep, just like that.

All the way down, down, down, down, down, down, down and let your conscious self concentrate on something. In fact let your conscious self do its very best to begin reliving, say, the last best Chelsea game that you saw or that you heard about, or anything related to that. Let's make it something that you've seen that was really good.

Let your conscious self begin to relive that particular sort of thing and hold onto it for as long as it takes until you find yourself come to full consciousness again.

Just find that your conscious self thinks about that game and only that game until all the thoughts about that game get so big that that's absolutely the only thing that can possibly occupy your conscious mind.

And as you do that let your unconscious self come a little close, pay a little more attention to my voice, although I believe you've already done a fantastic job of becoming very good at becoming closer and opening up.

I'm going to give you a suggestion you can do when you're wide awake, and we can do this from now on if you think it would be good, if you think it would be useful, I think it can be. This is something that Lady R'uetha likes to do. In addition to having people say "Green, green, green, green" if something is good, she says "Tell me something I need to know" so let's have you find yourself–when you come up–telling me something I need to know.

And then we can go from there. In the meantime, find yourself wide awake the instant I snap my fingers, right now.

DJ:  Why was I thinking about the Chelsea game?

LA:  Which one?

DJ:  Chelsea-Arsenal, 6-0.

LA:  That's a good score, huh?

DJ:  It was.

LA:  I saw that picture you posted today.

DJ:  OK so they do it differently in Britain obviously. So they don't have playoffs to determine the champion, the champion is whoever wins the most points, but during the course of the season they have different cup competitions. So there's the FA cup and the league cup. The FA cup is the oldest competition to the soccer world and any organized team in England that is part of the big, giant pyramid can take part so even your local pub team can take part in it.

LA:  Yeah they send all the pub teams to play with each other and then whoever gets on gets the lowest teams, etc., etc.

DJ:  Yeah so it's a big knockout competition that I think there's now Arsenal and Hull are left right now. And then there is a league cup, and that's just the teams of the top four divisions. And that's also run concurrent with everything else.

LA: That's right, so I needed to know that?

DJ: ...didn't you ask??

LA: Well I'm just checking.

DJ: I don't know.

LA: All right. So let's do the next one.

DJ: My brain's working in the background on something...

LA: Is it?

DJ: ...it's not coming up with anything.

## Notes

DJ: It's slightly difficult to judge the efficacy of this particular method; the 'secret' command was fairly amorphous. Here I was asked to tell Lee things she might want to know. Which is something I think I'd do anyway as the subject to a hypnotist.

I will say that I have probably volunteered things sooner to Lee than I think I otherwise might have done (I usually like to mull things over a bit before I talk about them to my friends), but whether that's from this suggestion is unclear.

Regardless, in my sparse notes from the session, I barely mentioned this experiment and barely knew if anything had happened. I certainly didn't recall her mention of Lady R'uetha.

# CHAPTER NINE

## *Experiment 9 Going Through a Door*

**Swing open; walk through**
**Embrace what spreads before you**
**(Let go what's behind.)**

This method is derived from fairly conclusive scientific studies regarding what happens to the human psyche when a person walks through a door. Somehow, changing rooms by leaving through a doorway changes one's perception. It serves as an interrupt from what one was thinking prior to the room change.

Our human experience almost certainly backs this up. Have you ever been looking for something, like your purse, or set of keys, or glasses? You search the room you're in and you don't see them. So you proceed to the next room and... you forget what you're looking for.

There is something psychologically relevant about switching rooms that impacts the capacity to remember, sometimes making it more difficult for the person switching rooms.

This method tries to take advantage of this fact, by having the subject first think of an object, and then imagine they are switching rooms, and seeing what happens.

As you will read, there were some initial hiccups, but we think we still demonstrated the effect.

LA:   So DJ deep sleep, that's right, all the way back down again. Deeper and deeper and deeper, and this time as you find yourself sinking so effortlessly into trance, more easily, more deeply—your unconscious mind finds itself remembering what I say about finding yourself always sinking more fully, more deeply, perhaps more intensely into trance.

And yet still finding your unconscious mind always at the most suggestible level no matter how deeply in trance you go you always find yourself at that most suggestible level for me.

And then while you're there dropping down, sinking deeper and deeper, I'd like you to take a piece of information and all you have to do with that piece of information is remember to hold onto it, but maybe it isn't where you are right now, it's some other place and that's OK.

Right now you're thinking that when you get to this other place you have this thing that you need to do and in the meantime you can feel like you're almost moving around through whatever space you're in.

And then you go through a door, are you in the space you need to be in? I don't know. You look around, it's different, the instant you stepped through that door something probably changed, whether it's a new view or something else, I don't know. You go through the door and all of a sudden your senses are aware of new things, sounds, smells, sights, maybe it's colder or warmer than the other door.

Maybe you had to touch a doorknob to get there or the lights in this room when you get to this space, I don't know. Maybe the weather is different, I don't know what it is, and then let's go through another door, through another space, and another to another space to another, and at some point in time we might find ourselves, you might find yourself in that space where you have to do something.

But go ahead and find yourself going through another door, and another space and another door, and another space, and another door and you turn left as you go through it.

And then another door, and you go up the stairs this time, and another door, and you keep going straight this time, and then another door, and another, and all the way up NOW! *Snap!* [Slight pause.]

Can you remember the thing that you were supposed to do, that you might have done?

DJ: No.

LA: Do you remember anything about that?

DJ: No?

LA: I don't think I did that one quite clearly enough. I should have asked you a question at some point in time and I didn't so...

Deep sleep.

All the way right back down, and as you find yourself dropping back into that very deep place, as soon as you think of something that you might need to do whether its say grab your keys, whether it's pick up your phone off the charger, whether it's pick up a book, whether it's grab something you have to give somebody.

When you have a thing you can do in another space just let your hand lift up and touch your chin and drop back down. Thank you.

And then leave that room and go through a door. Then another one, turn right this time as you leave this one. Go down the stairs, through another door on your left, go straight into another room.

Exit the room through another door, through another door, and all the way up on five. One, two, three, four, five.

So now do you remember that thing?

DJ: I was supposed to grab something.

LA: Do you remember what it was though?

DJ: I think so?

LA: Well I don't know because I didn't ask you to tell me what it was so...

DJ: Right.

LA: I think I may not be explaining this one very well, however I generally don't use it in that particular context, I usually use it in a context of not having you specifically remember something that then that act of going through the door would cause you to forget. But usually...?

DJ: For example what...?

LA:  Well usually what I would do is something along the lines of… have you do whatever I'm going to have you do in the audio, perhaps install a trigger for later, and not have you remember something specific like that. I did ask your unconscious if it had something so I might have thrown it off a little bit.

DJ:  Keys!

LA:  What?

DJ:  They were keys.

LA:  Oh, right, they were keys! Yes, I may have to find a better way to make that happen. As in, I may have to find a better trance thing that isn't "Remember this kind of thing" and then see how that goes.

DJ:  And it might be one of those things where you have to, you know, maybe do three different things that are at hand and then you choose one of those that I am going to forget when I walk through the door.

LA:  It might be or it might be along the lines of a whole bunch of different options and then I ask you something like "Did you remember to do this?" and you're like "I don't know."

### Notes

DJ:  Despite the slight confusion with the process, I did in fact find this to be fairly effective. The item in question was my keys both times, and it wasn't until Lee had implicitly given me permission to remember them that the word and the object popped back in to my head.

In my notes from that day, I wrote the following:

*First time wasn't as effective for the reasons we discussed; there was no 'fact' discussed to forget. The act of it (being sent through different doors, etc.) was really interesting and acted as a kind of confusion induction in and of itself.*

*Curious how this might work in a live setting (actually telling someone they will forget something specific when they walk through a door).*

*It seems to me that the words associated with this method (go through a door, go down a hall, turn left, etc.) would very much be a confusion induction or deepener of sorts. To me, it almost felt like a trance inside of a trance.*

# CHAPTER TEN

## *Experiment 10 Scopolamine*

**It's called Devil's Breath;**
**Blanks the mind, leaves you open**
**Such a perfect drug.**

Scopolamine Trigger

Scopolamine is a drug that has been used for decades as a treatment for motion sickness and nausea. It is made from the "Nightshade" family of plants (including Jimson weed and Henbane) and has been known to scientists for quite a long time. It also has more nefarious uses and has also been known as the "Zombie drug," or "Hell's breath."

As a non-medicinal drug, it induces both amnesia and suggestibility.

It has prominently been used in Colombia by gangs to reportedly steal from unwitting victims. The story is that the bandit will blow some powder in the victim's face, and then the victim is 'easily led.' There are (possibly apocryphal) stories of a person waking up after two days to find that their entire apartment has been emptied. When asking the doorman what happened, the doorman replied that the victim had helped the thieves leave with all of his possessions.

As you can imagine, a drug with the power to induce both amnesia and suggestibility is the perfect means to test hypnotic amnesia. The writers here take pains to note that overdosing with Scopolamine can lead to heart attacks and death, and that it is a controlled substance. Implanting a "Scopolamine" post-hypnotic trigger, on the other hand, is perfectly legal.

Here, Lee implanted just such a trigger.

LA: Deep sleep! Right down, all the way down, down, down, down. I've talked about exactly how Scopolamine works, and you've read that little thing from the internet about how it strips you of your free will. Of course there are debates going on as to whether humans have free will anyway, and of course we may have it on a limited basis but think about what it's like as I tell you about Scopolamine again so you can take it and not even know because it can be ingested, it can be sunk in through the skin, it can be breathed in, or drunk.

When the Scopolamine hits your system it makes you very compliant, it makes you very open to suggestion. Somebody else's will becomes the thing that you do.

It also prevents your unconscious mind from forming short-term memories, or prevents you from forming short-term memories and so you do these things that are suggested to you happily, willfully, cheerfully, excitedly. I don't know if you'll be cheerful and excited, but certainly willing, you do these things willingly and with no memory that you've done them afterward.

Now depending on what was done you might realize something had been done, but you wouldn't know what it was because you wouldn't have a memory of that. So let's say, because I don't want to use this on a heavy duty basis, if your unconscious mind gets the idea behind Scopolamine use and knows that that state is something that could be fun to use for the purposes of our book writing and when agreed upon ahead of time, later and only then, and again when it's as safe and appropriate as possible, is your unconscious mind OK with giving you the experience of having taken Scopolamine with me–let's say with me only–under those specific guidelines and only if I say… let's see what's a good word for you or a good phrase might be… "Scopolamine time now."

If your unconscious mind is OK with the concept as I laid out and it's OK responding to that trigger, whether you're deeply in trance or wide awake, please just let one of your hands rise up and touch your chin, and let me know that that is a yes. Thank you.

So wake up NOW! *Snap!*

I think that I just have a really good time with waking you up suddenly anyway.

DJ: And why is that?

LA: I don't know there's something about that I find very entertaining where you're like "Ah…"

DJ: Well like I said, Wiseguy did break off in mid-sentence and say 'what a nice expression.'

LA: Yeah.

DJ: …Yeah.

LA: I'm going to order some of his books and send them to the Netherlands, my friends over there are reading a book right now that they are complaining about the grammar and other things, and I'm not sure that his grammar is 100% better but I think it's going to be better than some other things, so I'm going to send it for their group.

DJ: I may need to pick some up to see what the competition is like.

LA: Well, it's not competition.

DJ: I know, I know.

LA: It's just different.

DJ: To see what the literature out there is like.

LA: Yeah, I like to do it also to support the local community. And I definitely think the e-book version there should be a "And you've completely forgotten you have this kindle version if at any time you plan to put this out onto any sort of message board." I'm just saying…"And you'll contact the authors and let them know what you've tried to do and you may not know you've done it but they will remember."

DJ: I like it. "You may not think this will work but can you take that chance?"

LA: That's right. So…

DJ: I have a vague recollection that there is a trigger, but I noticed that you didn't do an end trigger.

LA: Oh that's because I figured that I would simply end the time like I would do something else, like "All gone" or something like that.

I didn't figure it would need it's own end because it probably would have an end that would just get said. I'm a big fan of "All gone." And that way

66

since it's kind of generic and it works with so many things I don't actually have to tell you what the trigger is.

Like I can say "Pause" and then "Release" but I don't have to do that with this one because it will just work. Although, now I am thinking about the best time and place to use that kind of thing.

[From the next session.]

LA: We could certainly do "Scopolamine Time Now." And that would be a really interesting thing. I'm not exactly sure what sorts of things you might find yourself doing. However, I guess what would be more interesting to me right now, I guess, because you should actually feel normal. That's the whole point of this thing. That you kind of feel normal. And there's just other stuff going on in your head. Now, I'm not certain how compliant you feel, and you may find yourself feeling absolutely defiant, that's certainly a possibility, but... OK. Take your shirt off.

[DJ Takes his shirt off.]

All right, so you have two, and so it's not really a big deal. And I'm not the kind of person who makes other people strip. However, sometimes it's entertaining. I don't think I've ever told you about "Yes."

DJ: [With a slightly dreamy voice.] No.

LA: [Laughs.] "Yes" is a very powerful suggestion. I'll tell you how "Yes" goes. But I'll tell you why I mention the thing about the shirt. I mention the thing about the shirt because, sharing with someone that I work with as a subject and their hypnotist, I said there's this thing I do called "Yes," which makes people compliant. As long as I ask them a question in a certain specific way the answer is always "Yes." And I asked them if they would like me to do this with them. And they said "Sure, that would be great." So I put them in a trance. Now I think you're in an altered enough state so that your unconscious mind will just pick up how this works. And here's how it goes.

From now on, whenever I–and only I–ask you a question that begins with "Wouldn't you," "Don't you," or ends with something like, "Right?" or "Isn't that true," or something along those lines, where it's clear that the answer that the answer I'm looking for is a "Yes," you automatically find yourself doing that. And you automatically find yourself doing that because your unconscious mind thinks about it and realizes that it already thought about that exact same thing at some point in the past and came up with the conclusion that "Yes" is the right answer, so it just says "Yes." Every single time you say "Yes," it feels really good. Every single time you say yes, it makes every next "Yes" that much easier. Every single time you say yes, if it's something that you can make happen, you simply find that you do.

DJ: This is one of your "Siren's Spell" file suggestions?

LA: Yes. So you've experienced this before, haven't you?

DJ: Yes.

LA: Then, of course, if you think about saying "No," your unconscious mind stops you in place, which your unconscious mind is very good at doing, thinks about it, realizes that it's thought about it and realizes that "Yes" is of course the right answer. Your mouth says "Yes" because you've said it, it automatically becomes more true, and you find that you can move again.

So that's how yes goes. So you have heard it in "Siren's Spell" and let's say…?. All gone!

DJ: [DJ looks around, and seems slightly bleary-eyed.]

I'm not wearing my shirt!

LA: That's true!

DJ: [Laughs a long belly laugh.] Oh, this is so much fun.

LA: I wonder, and you don't remember our conversation about "Yes," do you?

DJ: Were we talking about the band?

LA: No.

DJ: OK… OK. I didn't think we would be. Then I guess not. It feels like there was a pane of glass that's slightly opaque that dropped in front of me. Like if I *really* concentrated on it I could probably remember it, what we did.

LA: It would be really useful that if you focused on it, the opaqueness of the glass. And then the closer you got to it, the more the glass itself would just seem to engage your vision. You'd notice the little flecks in the glass, the depth of the glass, the frosting, and that would be it. And that would be fine.

DJ: Yes.

LA:   And yes… your shirt is off.

DJ:   Yes it is.

LA:   And so… You actually took it off very quickly. And so, you know, my point wasn't… like really quickly.

DJ:   OK… were we doing the Scopolamine trigger?

LA:   Yes, you said we hadn't done the trigger yet, had we? And I was like, now is as good a time as any.

## Notes:

DJ:   This is the entirety of my notes from the session:

*Will have to wait for the transcript for sure; this is where the amnesia really started kicking in. I think there was something about the 'high concept' of it that really appealed to my brain; it felt eager to play along, if that makes sense. The 'shock' of finding my shirt on the ground was really enjoyable.*

I believe we have played around with the trigger a little bit since the recording. Each time I remember nothing when the trigger is given. At most I have a vague recollection of smiling just after the trigger is given and then…? Nothing until the trigger is called off.

# CHAPTER ELEVEN

## *Experiment 11 Short-Term Memory*

### *Blink and you miss it*
### *Stare and you might recover*
### *It's gone in a flash*

Here we have an interesting experiment because it plays with different *types* of memory. Here, the subject is told to empty out the 'short-term' memory banks. Whatever happens since a particular point is now no longer accessible. However, the memory is 'allowed' to enter the 'long-term' memory banks. We'll see in the notes how that worked in practice.

DJ:   [Coughs.]

LA:   OK, deep sleep. Down deeper, deeper, deeper.

Notice how good you can feel as you slide down into that trance state as you feel yourself getting so comfortable, as you feel yourself sliding down there mentally and physically.

Everything about that just making you feel so very good, and as you find yourself dropping down more and more and more deeply down into trance this one takes the Scopolamine part of it and does something different with it.

So this is what I'd like you to do for that... I'm going to ask your unconscious mind to find the place where it stores your short-term memories and as soon as it's found the place where your short-term memories are stored I'd like you to just touch your chin for me and please remember that I am recording this so you'll have both a recording at your disposal and a transcript at your disposal so you can always know what happened at this point in time.

70

I just want to make sure you're completely comfortable with this.

[DJ touches his chin.]

Thank you, and will you from the moment that you coughed–and only from then until I wake you up–make sure that your unconscious mind empties that short-term memory out and lets it stay blank?

Your unconscious mind can take this information I'm sharing with you and send it directly to your long-term memory or it can send it directly to another space that your unconscious has access to only, and you can process it tonight when you sleep… however you normally do, but I'm asking you to keep it empty until I wake you up and if that's something you can agree to do please just touch your chin again for me and will do.

[DJ touches his chin.]

Thank you.

I don't know what it's going to feel like; if it will feel different or if you will feel anything at all. But in the meantime go ahead and just sink down more deeply:

Number seven, the color blue, the sound of frogs, any one of those things. I don't need you to forget those things.

I just need you to have no short-term memory from the time that you coughed last until I wake you up on the count of five right now.

One, two, three, four, five wide awake.

DJ:  I think I was just in a trance.

LA:  You do?

DJ:  Yes.

LA:  Why do you think that?

DJ:  Uh, good question. I don't know.

LA:  Do you have that yummy feeling?

DJ:  A little bit. But then I had that for most of the day or at least most of the last hour.

[Lee and DJ moved on to another experiment.]

## *Notes*

DJ: There are very few notes from this session:

*Waking up and then having the memory of what happened was a very unusual feeling. It felt like a deleted scene being restored. Will have to review the transcript to see if I remembered everything.*

It's very strange to read the transcript and remember everything that happened, so to speak. But I also recall at the time not remembering that this session happened at all. In fact, it was only after waking up the next day that I remembered that we had done this.

LA: Memory is formed and stored in all our senses, the important things are processed at night while we sleep, through images and stories, perhaps even our dreams, so that they're there for our long-term recall. Once we recall a memory, however, we have irrevocably changed it. Most memories are not that reliable. When we 'send' a memory directly to long-term storage, we're telling the unconscious that it's important, and to please make sure it's available for recall later, no matter how precise that recollection ends up being!

# CHAPTER TWELVE

## *Experiment 12 Rewind*

**Intertwined notions**
**Still or sent back in your time**
**Notions intertwined.**

With this method we start to move into more advanced techniques for hypnotic amnesia. Here, the subject is asked to go back to a certain point in time, as if the previous few minutes hadn't actually happened. At this point, it is really up to the hypnotist what to do with the subject, whether to treat it as a reset or 'do over' or whether to, essentially, see if the subject will merely repeat the same things over and over again given the same stimulus. DJ had issues at first, but we think it will be instructive how the pair overcame the issues.

LA:  DJ, deep sleep. That's right. Just sink right back down. Effortlessly dropping and sinking down more and more deeply. [Laughs.] Part of me is tempted to add on more things because when you add multiple amnesia things on top of each other it can be even more effective. But in the meantime, just go ahead and sink and drop. As your unconscious mind comes a little closer and takes you to that place where you are as wonderfully open to my suggestion as you ever have been, this is how your mind works, so for from now on, when I–and only I–say to you "DJ, rewind" and some number of minutes, or "Rewind to" some event, your unconscious mind automatically takes you back there. And it automatically takes you back there, and you just start over from that point in time. Whether you're actually starting over or starting fresh is to be determined but your unconscious mind just carries on as though that period of time never actually happened, and you might notice–well, I've certainly noticed—that sometimes the conversations can be similar. But sometimes they're very different. And so whether it's twenty minutes, or an hour, you'll notice that your unconscious mind gets very good at the whole rewinding process.

There is a flip side to this called "Fast forwarding." It doesn't quite do the opposite. Because it can't quite do the opposite. What it could do is either allow your unconscious mind to have your conscious perceive that time as correct, only it stretches out the activities that have happened, and to fill that time or for your unconscious to create things that have happened in that period of time. Either one is OK.

And of course I might say to you "Remember that we did this," and your unconscious mind might go "Oh yeah, sure we did this." And fill it in, the details, for your conscious self.

Anti-amnesia? I'm not sure. But in the meantime, let your unconscious mind think about how it will accomplish that "Rewind" for you when I say "DJ, rewind ten minutes," or "Rewind until" a certain event. Let your unconscious mind think about how it's going to make that happen. And as it thinks about how it's going to make that happen and it knows that it can and that it will, just go up and reach for your chin again, and as you scratch your chin, notice that you can come back all the way up. Once that's fully engaged in your systems.

So. I don't want to use that too much right now. Because we've already done some amnesia stuff. And I don't want to get you stuck in a place where that might be. But I can say to you, for example, "Rewind to just before I said 'Deep Sleep.'"

[Lee laughs as DJ blinks for a few seconds.]

DJ:   What?

LA:   Nothing.

DJ:   Are you having fun?

LA:   I am having fun, thank you.

DJ:   OK, good.

LA:   All right, so shall we do "The Harder You Try to Remember, the More Quickly It Fades Away?"

DJ:   [Pause.] Uh… does that mean we've done the "Rewind"

LA:   Yes. Yes it does.

DJ: ...sure, why not? [Shakes head.]

LA: [Laughs.] OK. And this is why we record this.

DJ: Yes. Good. My notes after this are going to be very slight.

## Notes

DJ: Indeed. The notes for this entire day started to be very 'slight.' Here are the notes for this experiment:

*Will have to review the transcript, again. I have no memory of doing this.*

Today, even reading the transcript, I have to take the recording's word (so to speak) that it happened.

LA: I've used this trigger for years, in one audio of mine, Dark Side Sticky, and in sessions. One client in particular was highly adept at rewind—they could rewind so completely that after an hour session, if I rewound it, their clock (to them) would read the time we began the session, 60 minutes prior, and consciously they'd have zero recollection that we'd had the session until I allowed it. What other uses can you think of that this might be practical or fun in?

# CHAPTER THIRTEEN

## *Experiment 13 The Harder, The Faster*

> ***Try to remember.***
> ***Go ahead now, really think.***
> ***Thought's then gone so fast.***
>
> ***The more you squeeze tight***
> ***The more memories will slip***
> ***Through grasping fingers***

The harder you try to remember, the more quickly what you tried to remember fades away. This experiment installs a trigger that makes the very act of *trying* to remember the trigger for spurring the amnesia itself.

This is certainly a trigger for the more devious-minded hypnotist.

In the transcript, note how Lee changes the triggers on the fly, and manages to extend the efficacy of the trigger beyond its initial use.

Also included here is the conversation Lee and DJ had regarding some other aspects of hypnotic amnesia play.

DJ: So "The Harder You Try to Remember, the More Quickly It Fades Away."

LA: Yeah. [Laughs.]

DJ: For the record, Lee just laughed maniacally. OK. Not maniacally, more like evilly.

LA: Let's say, Deep Sleep. That's right. All the way down. Because everything about going all the way down becomes easier and easier, especially with all this fractionation. And you find yourself really capable of making happen, really effortlessly capable of making happen, right now over and over and

76

over again, the fractionation helps, you can drop and sink so many times, and in fact, this is what I'd like you to do right now, do I need you to do this right now, or do I need you to write something out? Um. All right. So I'm going to tell you something, I don't know what I'm going to tell you just yet. And part of you is really going to want to hold on to remembering what that is. And the other parts of you, all the other parts of you, are going to do what it takes to ensure that whatever the thing is that I told you, that it just quickly fades away, perhaps even as though all those other little parts of you are just taking a piece of that information and going [blows air] and blowing it far out of your mind, and it just feels like the harder you try to look, the harder you try to remember, and also, if at any point of time any part of you is tempted to just let it pop into your mind, when you're not really thinking about it, all of those things simply quickly, act to take that piece of information and just pop it out of your head. Let it fade away, let it go away, let it just disappear.

And everything about that begins to feel better and better and better. And so, what's the piece of information I'm going to share with you today? The piece of information I'm going to share with you right now is that NEST has been happening since 1997. And that doesn't really mean anything to you; you don't really have to know that. And it's something you could look up if you really needed to know it. Or if I were quizzing you. But because I've told you that that's the piece of information, that the harder you try to remember it, your unconscious mind simply lets it fade away very fast. Lets it be gone very fast. And notice how good it feels to let it happen. For you to drop and sink down deeper and deeper and deeper still, and then, on the count of five come back all the way. And if your unconscious mind agrees that the harder you try to remember the more quickly that fades away, you're going to touch your chin with your hand again. [DJ touches his chin.] One, two, three, four, five wide awake.

All right, so. How much of that do you remember?

DJ:  I remember… We, um… you got me under? …That's it.

LA:  That's very interesting.

DJ:  Yes?

LA:  I thought of a new thing to do as well. So, not just using overload, in terms of a lot of information and then maybe your brain remembers some of it and maybe it doesn't, but, also using pleasure overload? So, I like to have people have, some of the people I work with are very good at full body instant orgasms, and they can have them over and over and over and over. And over and over and over and over and over again.

DJ: [Laughs.]

LA: So I'll let their conscious-self focus on that, and then let everything else just go through, and those are very good amnesia sessions.

DJ: I'm sure.

LA: I think that the act of having 20 even full body orgasms in a row is pretty... You'd think it'd be pretty exhausting, but most people are still willing to have more. There's something about that that doesn't prevent them from wanting to have more orgasms. Which is good. So I added that to number 15—I added "Pleasure Overload" to "Overload."

DJ: OK.

LA: So, you don't remember at all?

DJ: You know... uh. No.

LA: OK.

DJ: Funnily enough, the more I try to remember, the faster it goes away. Go figure.

LA: Yeah. Go figure.

DJ: It's a little frustrating.

LA: Yeah. But it might be more frustrating if I said the more you try to remember the slower it goes away, but you still can't remember it. Wouldn't that be frustrating in a very fun way?

DJ: [Laughs.] Yes.

LA: So we could do "Harder 1" and "Harder 2." And your brain can just assimilate the "Harder 2" bit that I just put in there. Just like that.

DJ: Just like that.

LA: [Laughs.] You know. Not everyone's brain does that. I just want to tell you that. I mean, I feel really lucky to work with people's brains that do that. So I think your brain is rapidly becoming the kind of brain that is as suggestible in the right circumstances as it can be so that your unconscious is in this place where you're really open to having those processes in your head just created or adjusted. Which is really pretty powerful. I mean, really pretty powerful.

DJ: As you're saying that, I get that yummy trance-y feeling. So... Yes.

LA: Yes. Excellent. Good job, brain.

DJ: Yay, brain!

If you had asked me to forget a piece of information–because I think there's a piece of information you gave me, which I think I got yesterday?– from a different source. Maybe...? maybe not. (slightly confused)

LA: You could find that information out again. I'm certainly not saying it's necessary for you to know the information constantly. I bet there will be a time when you stumble back upon the information you found out about yesterday and there it is. And that would be just fine. I'm not saying you shouldn't know it. I'm just saying that for the purposes of that particular demonstration, not being able to remember it is exactly right. Now, on the other hand I could say to you, so remember it now. And you do.

DJ: Yes. NEST was founded in 1997.

LA: And if I said to you "Harder 2" *Snap!*. Then what happens?

DJ: It... [Laughs.] I was about to say something about what it was, but now I don't remember what it was.

LA: Very nice. And so I guess one of the beautiful things about amnesia, and admittedly, we've been working on this, so there's an advantage to us because we *have* been working on it, is that people can know that amnesia is capable of being done on the fly like that. 'Cause I didn't put you into a trance, I gave you a totally new way to do something, and you both assimilated the new way to do it and the amnesia happened, without you being in an additional trance state. Again, you still may be slightly fractionated, even though we've only done a few things for the past 45 minutes or so.

DJ: Well, essentially, it's not really a post hypnotic trigger, because you did it while I was in a conscious state, albeit a suggestible state.

LA: Yeah. True. Another fascinating, fascinating thing about suggestion.

DJ: You don't have to be in a trance to be suggestible.

LA: No. Not at all.

## Notes

DJ:  Here are the notes from the following day:

*The memory finally came back sometime this evening, for what it's worth. This is the first time it felt seriously like something was being done 'to me' as opposed to 'with me.' It felt like my whole body was responding, as opposed to just my mind.*

*I'm very intrigued by how much my mind has been enjoying playing in this way, and how far it's come. I'm definitely intrigued by playing with some of the first methods now that my brain has been 'trained' this much.*

*Also, I find it amusing that I have less and less to review afterward, since I'm forgetting more and more. All in all, I'm having more and more fun with this.*

I should note that this is probably not for subjects who do not enjoy being frustrated on some level. The very notion that my brain was hiding something from me, and being more and more effective at it the more I tried to remember, was, for me, a fantastic feeling. But I can totally see how someone else might find that a deal-breaker.

# CHAPTER FOURTEEN

## *Experiment 14 Right Feeling, Wrong Info, and False Memories*

***Truthiness at work;***
***This is a perfect haiku***
***You've got the idea***

This experiment goes in a slightly different direction. This method doesn't ask the subject to technically 'forget' the information in question. Instead, it encourages the mind to think about the feeling one gets when the subject feels a 'right' answer. All of us have that moment when our mind reaches out and recognizes that a piece of information 'answers' the question correctly.

Well, what happens if we take that feeling, and associate it with an 'incorrect' answer? Then the mind is 'tricked' into thinking that the 'incorrect' answer is 'correct.' In essence, the subject will 'forget' the correct information and insist that an answer is right, even when it is palpably wrong.

This can be a way of achieving effects extremely similar to amnesia, as we see here.

This kind of method, along with implanting actual false memories, as here, comes with two notes of caution:

First, it challenges the abilities of the hypnotist. It may be obvious, but is worth stating explicitly that it is extremely helpful for the hypnotist to know something of the subject's history, so as to have the idea of an event to play with. Also, once an event or thing is chosen, the hypnotist needs to craft something that is within the bounds of reason and believability. As we'll see in the demonstration transcript below, Lee accidentally chose something that was beyond the bounds of believability for DJ's unconscious. The hypnotist can choose something that is, perhaps, bizarre or out-of-the-ordinary, but go too far, and you're likely to hit some resistance of some form or another.

81

Second, the hypnotist also needs to be careful that the memory being played with or inserted is not important to the subject for some reason, or in any way attached to some deep-seated emotional feeling. For example, (unless clearly negotiated in advance) we'd recommend staying clear of any insertions of memories related to partners or spouses, money issues, or any kind of fraught emotional territory. Likewise, we should reiterate, that the play we are recommending is on the premise of steering clear of anything even remotely related to therapy. It may seem like a good idea to relieve a subject of a painful memory, but such an action could have serious unintended consequences. This is one area where we recommend playing in the shallow end of the pool.

Note also how Lee incorporates one of the other methods to reinforce a suggestion to make *this* method more effective.

LA:  Deep sleep. That's right. Just all the way down. Right now, now, now, now, now. Feel how good it is to let that feeling of going into trance just invade your body right now. Taking every little bit of your mind with it. And as you find yourself dropping and sinking deeper down still, feel quickly you can go into that deepest level of trance, that you are in during one of the last couple of times. And as you go there and as you get really comfortable, a couple other things are going to be going on. So this is probably going to be a little challenging for your unconscious mind. As you drop down very, very, very deeply. So I'd like your unconscious to send your conscious self as far out of the way as possible. And to let my words slide into your unconscious. Perhaps to let a little bit of the sound of my voice hit your conscious self on some level, but really, just the barest little bit. Just enough so that maybe you notice that I'm talking, and maybe you don't quite know if I'm talking. And as your unconscious makes that happen, just reach up and touch your chin, and then let your hand fall taking you even more deeply into trance.

Thank you.

So this is what I'd like your unconscious mind to do right now. I'd like your unconscious mind to take this piece of information I'm about to give you, and then to spin a complete plausible and, on top of the plausibility, this complete understanding, and every part of you it needs to, in your eyes, your ears, your nose, your mouth, your skin…in your gut. As you think about what I'm going to tell you, I'd like you to create the rationalization for this, in every single realistic way possible. And when I give you the opposite piece of information when you're conscious, you're going to find you're going to protest the thing I told you that you're going to create the story for. To find yourself firmly, absolutely, committed to that story. Until I tell you to have the correct information back. So this is what I'd like you to commit yourself to right now. Please and thank you.

Even though, you worked for the Obama campaign, for whichever election you choose, you mistakenly and accidentally voted for Romney, and you didn't realize it until it was too late to get your ballot back. And as your unconscious mind can make the story and rationalize that particular story, just go ahead and reach up and touch your chin, and let your hand fall back again.

[Long pause. DJ does not touch his chin.]

I know that I'm asking a lot of you. But I still believe that your unconscious mind can make this happen, in a way that your conscious self is going to be incredibly committed to and absolutely believe. And, you know, this is for science.

[Another pause, DJ touches his chin.]

So, as soon as your unconscious mind knows that your conscious self is going to commit itself to that story as completely as possible–in fact, you might find the need to tell me about it when you come up?–just find yourself wide, wide awake.

[Pause, DJ wakes up.]

DJ:   Puppet on a string.

LA:   [Laughs.] Because you go down into trance so easily?

DJ:   [Laughs.] Yes. Oh, so, one of the embarrassing things about the 2012 election was that… we had set up in advance that we were going to go to Vegas, to do this thing, so we had to vote absentee. And I'll never know for sure, because I did it by mail, and I don't really have a record of it, but I remember going over the ballot afterward, and I swear… [There's a pause here.]

I…might… have checked the wrong box for President.

LA:   Really?

DJ:   It's possible.

LA:   So you voted for Romney.

DJ:   Now! Look! See! I… I… I didn't say that.

LA:   Well, I'm trying to clarify what you are saying.

DJ:   I'm saying that I… uh… that it's possible… that I may not have voted for the guy who won. Accidentally. That I may have voted for his main challenger, on accident. But I'll never know for sure because, of course, like I said, they don't keep records of those things.

LA:   Right.

DJ:   But I… recall that I, I, I, think I… because it's all at the top of the ballot, and the way the numbers work out is that, like, Obama was number one and Romney was number two, and I think I marked the wrong number on the ballot.

LA:   Maybe an even number just appealed to you at that time.

DJ:   S-sure. That's an excuse. Other than being an idiot.

LA:   No, no. Have all the information back.

DJ:   Oh, for god's sakes!

LA:   [Laughs evilly and for a really long time.]

DJ:   [Gets up from his seat and walks around. Pounds things on his desk. Has a mini-temper tantrum.]

LA:   [Continues to laugh.]

DJ:   God dammit.

LA:   [Laughs some more.]

DJ:   You're just so happy with yourself right now, aren't you?

LA:   No! I'm laughing because your response was so 180.

DJ:   [Laughs.]

LA:   Because you were so rational before and a little apologetic and all of sudden you're all "Oh, hell no!"

[Both laugh.]

DJ:   I'm embarrassed. There was a part of me underneath going, "No. No! Stop this. This is wrong! No. Stop!"

LA: Here's the thing, I think that it's... I'm glad that your brain is doing that, but I think it's possible not just...

[Brief pause for water.]

I just have this feeling, what if, instead of spending another ten or fifteen minutes on something like that, we were working together on that one thing for a few days? Even that part of you that's going, "No, no, no, no, no!" could be silenced. Could be made to just stop protesting. And maybe that part of you that is protesting... in fact, I bet if I had said, "Let's have any part of you that's protesting simply let your unconscious mind totally turn the volume on that part of you all the way down," for example. So I guess if something like that were added in it would make a huge, huge difference. If you don't have any part of you that on any feeling, hearing, sight level is giving you conflicting stuff, unless some part of you interpreted that as "No, no, no, you really did vote for the wrong thing."

DJ: Right. Those protests that you're hearing in your brain are just the protests that of you not accepting that you did that.

LA: As a hypnotist, you don't always know what people are thinking or what they might do. So, for example, instead of that, if I said, "DJ, rewind five."

And then I say, DJ, "Forget switch on." And just go ahead and have that part of you that was saying "No," and being loud, just let it get turned all the way down, and if you hear any of those voices it's just the protests that you shouldn't have done it, but you did it anyway. And when I finish talking and you can remember again, you can go to that same spot in the story. Forget switch off.

DJ: So, it was really embarrassing that I voted that way.

LA: Well, you'll probably never do that again.

DJ: Well, at least I made up for it by going to Vegas and working on the campaign. I like to think I saved a bunch of votes by doing that. So it's not like he was going to lose California anyway. So, in that sense, it really didn't make a difference. But still, probably the only time I voted for that particular party in my entire life. On a presidential level, anyway.

LA: OK. You can have all of that back again.

DJ: [Audible sigh.]

LA: And... [Laugh.] So, that time how did feel?

DJ:  It felt easier.

LA:  I'm not sure if it's the second time around that makes it easier, or just in general. Was that voice quiet? The first time, you said...

DJ:  Um, yeah. It seemed a lot quieter. There was a sense of déjà vu, like, "This is embarrassing why are we still talking about this?"

LA:  Oh, I'm so sorry.

DJ:  No, no, no.

LA:  You know, I really like to delve deeply into things that are embarrassing to people, so we can have better experiences together. [Laughs.]

DJ:  [Laughs.] Is *that* how that works?

LA:  Well, sometimes.

DJ:  I wrote down, "So that worked."

There was definitely more of a sense of a playing along aspect to it. But it was definitely in the sense of, if I wanted to concentrate and broken through, I probably could have gotten there, but, I didn't feel like it, because for our purposes.

LA:  So that's always an interesting thing to me, because over the years, the most common thing I've heard when people are stopped in place for five minutes, is, "I felt like I could have moved, and I just didn't want to." So, I don't really know where the line is there. Because if you could do something and you just don't the results are that you didn't. And, when people are stopped in place with that particular trigger, their body is solidly still that they're not, if they're awake and simply holding their body in place. Because very few people are trained like mannequins and I'm willing to believe that they could do this. I also believe that human mannequins can benefit from hypnosis training. But, be that as it may. I think that people don't realize that if they try to hold themselves for ten seconds, or hold their hand perfectly straight, whatever, in strange positions, it just doesn't happen that same way. Does that mean that you're trying to justify not doing something? I don't know. But the result is...

There's often a lot of justification after the fact. And the bottom line ought to be "What did you do at the time?" At the time, did you remember, did you say, did you do, whatever?

DJ: I think that I'd be interested to see how different it would be if you had chosen something that wasn't so…

LA: So emotional? So powerful?

DJ: I was going to say as important, but yes. It's just one of those things where you just don't know what you're going to get until you work with that person what is important or emotional or powerful for them. I know for a lot of people, this would be fun to play with. For me it's like, "Romney was crazy and shouldn't be anywhere near the presidency. No way!"

LA: I thought it was interesting that you were embarrassed by that. And you didn't want to say his name, or—

DJ: Actually say the words, "I voted for Romney." Like how I never actually said *those* words. Because, in a million years, I never would have done that. Part of it is that I remember checking it like three times. Because I knew it was an absentee ballot. I was in the office of the Registrar making sure everything was all right. I went over the ballot three times just to make sure. Because it was so important to me it wasn't one of those throw away things. [It's not like] "I forget to pay my car registration on time."

LA: Right.

DJ: Because it was one of those important things–for me–was one of the reasons why I think it was a difficulty for me.

LA: Because I am already interested in amnesia to this particular extent that I am, I've never met anyone else who is quite as fascinated as I am, although you're probably getting there.

[Both laugh.]

LA: Part of me just wants to see how much more and the fun ways it can be used than I already know. It's not like I've made you forget something important.

DJ: …that I know of!

LA: [Laughs.] No. I'm pretty sure you'd remember. I mean, I'm pretty sure there are parts you don't remember because your notes are pretty terrible. [Laughs.]

"We did this, I think. I'm not sure."

DJ: [Laughs.] And they got worse over time, I know that.

LA: It'll be fine. I mean, I think you'll remember. I'm trying to have you remember more because I think it gives you a better ability to say something useful.

DJ: [Laughs.]

LA: And then, I don't know if you downloaded any of the audio files, by the way, but that's kind of fascinating that you'll get to rediscover those things.

DJ: I'm looking forward to it. I started listening to one of them, and it was classic how the sound of your own voice is so...?

LA: Weird?

DJ: It's like, oh. That's what I sound like.

Yeah, I'm looking forward to reading the transcripts, at least. At least the notes give a sense of what the feelings were like, even if they aren't particularly helpful in terms of detail or description.

[From a different session.]

DJ: How much of a burden does it put on you as a top/hypnotist in terms of being careful in terms of how you treat the subject?

LA: Generally speaking, I expect that the people I'm working with tend to be more suggestible to me than to anyone else. So, I'm not necessarily so concerned about someone that I work with having someone else come up to them and give them suggestions. I'm pretty sure they'd be like, "No, the walls are up, forget it. I'm looking through you, I see you. Don't do that again." I'm also fairly certain that I'm really careful about the things that I say most of the time. I tend to self-correct as necessary. I'm also really confident that my unconscious mind–when it talks to you–is talking to your unconscious self. Like all the time.

DJ: [Laughs.]

LA: I'm also pretty certain that my unconscious mind wants to have a good time, wants to get things done and might want to get things done with you and to you but only in the way that is going to be useful for you. Usually what I say is, "Good or fun, or both." So, I can pretty much tell when I've done something, that someone's brain has gone "Yes." I'm going to make that happen too. But not always, because the signs are a little more subtle, sometimes they're not quite there, but I work on being careful to give suggestions that are... wholesome? If that makes any sense?

DJ: Did you just say "Wholesome?"

LA: I did.

DJ: Please explain.

LA: I think these suggestions are going to be something that your brain can do that it will allow it to either expand its capabilities or expand on its current abilities and that it is something that your brain is going to enjoy doing. Because your brain enjoys it, and it enriches your competence, your intelligence, it then makes it happen. It is a beneficial skill for you to have, that sense of being 'wholesome.'

DJ: In a holistic sense that it is being that the entire person is going to accept and adapt and decide that it's a good idea.

LA: It's not a glass of milk wholesome. But it's not that far off.

There's that "So the 'Implant memories to supplant real ones' Experiment." I think it's almost like a therapeutic technique. I don't know if there's something that happened where you think, "I wish that had never happened." I don't necessarily want to get around to doing that, but we can talk about it. I mean, I'll talk about the ways in which I've used it. And it is really sort of powerful. I think all of these are powerful. But I think this one is powerful in a way that you want to be careful about. Like, I don't want to take somebody who's had a really traumatic life and implant a memory that overrides the old one and they won't remember the old one. And then again, maybe you do. But you don't want to put... I'm trying to think of the very best ways to make that happen. And sometimes, if you don't do it carefully, or if you haven't really thought about all the tendrils of the memory, which happened when I first started, you can get some resistance to it because it feels foreign. That's one reason to start out on things which are relatively unimportant, and not settled in the way an actual memory gets settled in. So for example, the friend that I'm working with that I made the video for yesterday, I was driving him back and he was reminding me that at some point in time I had tickled this other girl, and I remember a long time ago when we started he tried to get me to come out to Boston, to tickle her, and I just couldn't make my schedule match up with hers, and she couldn't make her schedule match with mine, so it never happened. But apparently, sometime in the last say five or six years, I actually did. He's trying to get me to remember the hotel room that we were in, and I was like, "You know, none of this is really coming back to me." Not any of it is coming back to me. So, you know, sometimes I have memories that I don't remember, and I suppose I could take something else and put it in that place, that was really vivid or a more vivid account of that and it may not actually have been true. My brain would have been like, "Oh, sure, I remember, she had this on, and I had that on," and whatever. You know what I mean. But there was nothing about it–and maybe I've had too many experiences and tickled too many people–there was nothing about it that made me go "Oh yeah. I totally remember her and that."

DJ: What is an example of something that you have done in the past where you've implanted a memory?

LA: In my audio, "Dark Side Love Dart," I allow people to pick a memory from their past, pick a place that they loved, and to recreate, basically… I don't do it, they do it themselves, they recreate an experience, and I give them an outline of it, and they can imagine all these things happening. Their brains do all the work, so they get this really strong feeling and memory, that they've actually done this thing, and it's not necessarily that its supplants anything else in their past life, I haven't done it in a way where it supplants anything else that way, what it does supplant is everything else that I'm telling them right then. Because while they are busy having that other experience in their brain with that other place that they love, with me, then their unconscious is paying attention to the other messages. Their unconscious is making those other messages really reinforce the feelings that they have from that memory that they're creating. Which is powerful of course. Maybe it's really powerful because they're creating it, like they're given the parameters and they're making it happen. As opposed to me saying, "This happened on this date in this place and you were wearing this," I don't have to do those really specific things, and I think it's really important to mention that because a lot of times hypnotists in general like to be so specific to a subject that it is often very disconcerting, it often takes them out of trance because that's not what they're seeing/hearing/feeling, etc. and it's not that you can't guide someone to that place, it's just that if you're guiding someone to that place, it's helpful if they can actually fill in the details themselves, and the little things you mentioned become just an effortless part of the whole thing. For our brain to go "Sure, why not?"

DJ: It reminds me of the movie "Inception," where the whole scene goes wrong because the one architect chooses the wrong carpet, and it's jarring. And I can see that, where, if you're going into too much detail, you know: what if I hate Mexico, why would I want to be on the beach in Cabo? As opposed to, "Imagine yourself in a place where you want to be."

LA:   Yeah. It's really funny, because some people have huge amounts of resistance to water. For a lot of people that is just like, forget it. I happen to love water. Do I have a fear of drowning? Probably a little bit. Do I have a fear of depths, because, there might be something in those waters that comes up and drags you down, and then you drown? Of course. I also have this fear of heights a little bit. So it's not that I won't jump off the high diving board but I won't dive off it, because I don't want that kind of experience. So I don't dive off the really tall diving board, but I'll jump off it. Because I don't want to conk my head or break my head and then drown. It doesn't stop me from going in the water, though. There's nothing about that that's too terrifying. I figured if I was going to die in the water it probably would have happened already.

So there are a lot of people who don't like all sorts of things, and allowing them to create something with a few guidelines is often helpful. And then sometimes you can get people over fears but that's not really in the scope of what we're doing. Although, we might get people over their fear of amnesia.

DJ:   Yes. Which is fine. For recreational hypnosis purposes, what would be the purpose of taking on a different memory?

LA:   OK. So, for example, you can use it for people who want to be a different gender. You can take them back in time to a birthday party they may have had, and turn it into a little girl's birthday party, instead of a little boy's birthday party. And from that moment you can have them come forward in life as though, when they were a child, their wish to have a little girl's party instead of a boy's, for example, got honored, and then to see how their life progressed. Do they grow out of it at some point? Does the new memory more firmly become supplanted in them? Those are both valid options. Some people feel so strongly about a gender, but because it's suppressed, because they're not allowed to be who they are, it gets even more firmly embedded inside, just like a lot of people with even more strongly embedded beliefs. You know, if a belief is mocked or made fun of, and denied, some people hold on to those really, really tightly. So, I think, both options, you might find someone who becomes really happy and healthy and enjoys being that, and all of a sudden one day decides to be something else, which is usually not a one day thing, usually their brain has been thinking about this for a really, really long time and goes "Oh, how about this today?" so it seems like it's brand new. Or they might just have decided "Hey, this is exactly right and it exactly fits me," and then go on and they can imagine what their life would be like with that support of the people around them, instead of whatever they wound up having, so it can be really useful in that sort of way. You can have people remember times when they had all the resources they could need to accomplish something, no matter what that something was. And you can do a little bit of regression with them, and let them re-imagine that experience or relive that experience with all those memories. And all of those resources. And notice what the difference would have been if they had done that. Oftentimes people come out of that feeling, really calm and really powerful. Or, at least, empowered.

DJ:   Right.

LA:   So it can be very useful to implant or adjust memories in that way.

DJ:   I assume you get some men who want to experience what it's like to be women, do you get many the other way?

LA:   No. I get zero that way. And it could just be that people don't want to come to me for that. And that's fine.

When I do that kind of thing, it's a transformation that I use NLP to work with, I use trance or a trance state, and it's really effective. I mean, it depends on the subject, of course, but it's a really effective place to find people in. And you can set it up as a trigger so that somebody can access it themselves for an hour or however long they really want to be that other thing, person, whatever it is.

I say "thing" because sometimes a lot of people like being animals and so I give them a suggestion that they can bring it on themselves.

DJ:   That's cool. I love hypnosis.

### Notes

DJ:   I felt so much like this is one topic where it felt more like I was 'playing along' than any other topic. The suggestion that I voted for Romney was so antithetical to my own beliefs, it definitely served as a litmus test of this method's efficacy. I'd be interested to try with something less 'fraught.' Regardless, I felt myself extremely willing to 'play along.' (I do find it interesting that I don't think I could bring myself to say the words "I voted for Romney," though.) The revelation, the flood coming in when I was told I could remember, was amazing! It felt like a dam had broken.

Either: (1) I am rationalizing after the fact and did not remember at the time, or (2) I was 'playing along' and improving under the suggestion, in which case, what is the effective difference?

The second time did also feel interesting from the perspective that it felt like déjà vu at the time. I felt better about the prospect of voting for Romney.

I was impressed with how my brain constructed a whole story for how I came to vote the wrong way so quickly. Again, when I was given leave to remember, both times, it was an amazing feeling; like an epiphany.

LA:   Humans are really amazing at rationalizing* behaviors; there's a particular case where a woman's arm is paralyzed from a stroke, and she justifies not using it by saying she was tired, or didn't want to lift it. Many people justify purchases after the fact by making them out to be (perhaps) more amazing products than they really are, or to justify why they purchased a more expensive thing than a cheaper one. When you realize that this is a fairly normal human behavior, it can be easy enough to allow someone's mind to come up with (to them!) a perfectly reasonable explanation for almost any behavior, as seen above.

* Rationalization definition as excerpted from Wikipedia here:

https://en.wikipedia.org/wiki/Rationalization_%28psychology%29

In psychology and logic, **rationalization** is a defense mechanism in which controversial behaviors or feelings are justified and explained in a seemingly rational or logical manner to avoid the true explanation, and are made consciously tolerable–or even admirable and superior–by plausible means.

Rationalization happens in two steps:

A decision, action, judgment is made for a given reason, or no (known) reason at all (in cases for instance of dogmatic judgment or normal behavior).

A rationalization is performed, constructing a seemingly good or logical reason, as an attempt to justify the act after the fact (for oneself or others).

Rationalization encourages irrational or unacceptable behavior, motives, or feelings and often involves ad hoc hypothesizing. This process ranges from fully conscious (e.g. to present an external defense against ridicule from others) to mostly unconscious (e.g. to create a block against internal feelings of guilt). People rationalize for various reasons --sometimes when we think we know ourselves better than we do.

# CHAPTER FIFTEEN

## *Experiment 15 Pleasure Overload*

*You feel good don't you?*
*How much pleasure can you stand?*
*Here, have more of it!*

*Pleasure, ecstasy,*
*Can overwhelm, fuck your mind*
*Terrible pity.*

This technique is probably one of the more enjoyable methods of distracting the mind. However, in order to truly take advantage of it, the hypnotist and subject should do some preparation work. (Certainly, if the relationship between hypnotist and subject is of the correct nature, more 'hands-on' techniques might work just as well.)

The central idea behind this technique is that the conscious mind is filled–overloaded–with pleasure, so much so that it either doesn't register the things being said to it, or is so suggestible it doesn't want to remember anything else.

The preparation work involves training the subject to experience a high level of pleasure based solely on triggers.

Lee likes to use a series of triggers called "Radio On." The trigger is used to instill a level of latent arousal in a person. She describes it as "A sense of being 'turned on' like a radio, but as if the radio were on in the background." So that, as DJ will attest, when the "Radio On" command is being used, the subject's body feels a dim, but very real, sense of arousal.

She will then tell the subject that the radio dial goes from one to ten, with ten being right on the brink of an orgasm. She will 'calibrate' the dial by walking the subject up from one to ten. When the subject is at ten, Lee will ask the subject whether they are truly on the brink of orgasm. If the subject is not, then she will designate that as five, or six, or whatever seems appropriate.

This will repeat several times until the subject can reach the brink of orgasm just by Lee saying "Radio on" and "Ten."

When Lee says "Orgasm Now!" the subject will have an orgasm.

Hypnotically-induced orgasms are not necessarily–for men–ejaculatory orgasms. DJ has said that they feel like an endorphin dump into the brain. They can be very sensual and erotic, or they can be a little like being hit with a sledgehammer.

Here, Lee uses this very trigger to get DJ up to, and over, the hypnotic finish-line, so to speak, and then to constantly trigger DJ to see if this alone can cause hypnotic amnesia.

LA: So is your unconscious mind ready to have lots and lots of orgasms? While your conscious self forgets all about everything else I'm doing in the meantime?

DJ: I'm going to give it a shot.

LA: Well, I don't really want your conscious mind's response to that, because I don't care about that.

So. Deep Sleep. *Snap!*

That's right. Just dropping into trance more completely. Just sliding and gliding and sinking down, and effortlessly dropping deeper and deeper, perhaps your unconscious self can take you right back right now to that place you were with the overload, thinking about those things and thinking about nothing else other than the sound of my voice, and just letting yourself get as comfortable as possible, as you need to for this session. And so that you'll be as comfortable when you find yourself coming back up, I'm going to ask you that question again: is your unconscious mind— because I want an unconscious response—ready to make sure that you can have lots and lots and lots of full body orgasms, right now in a way that prevents your conscious self from doing anything other than feeling that pleasure and hearing only the sound of my voice? And if it's a "Yes," you already know what I've been asking you to do for yes, so why don't you go ahead and do that again for me right now.

[DJ touches his chin.]

Thank you very much. Lovely. So find yourself dropping deeper and deeper and deeper. And, you know, some people don't actually like dropping deeper and deeper and deeper down. But I bet you can find yourself in a state of trance that's so completely intense and deep right now, as you find yourself going more fully there. Again. *Snap!*. And again. *Snap!*. And again *Snap!* and again *Snap!* this instant. *Snap!* Just like that. Deeper and deeper. Sliding down more fully right now.

Radio on. Let's start at five. And notice how very good five feels. But it's really irrelevant, how five feels. And let your conscious self feel the pleasure that comes from any of those numbers. From any of the orgasms. Deeper and deeper down. Because the important thing is that your conscious self gets to focus on six… how good it feels to hear those numbers get higher and higher and higher–six–and six, and six, and six, and six, and in fact let your conscious self–anytime I say a new number– simply keep repeating it on top of the sound of my voice, hear that number, whatever number we happen to be on, over and over and over again. About a second apart or so. As your unconscious mind simply takes up the rest of my suggestions and makes them your reality. Seven. And as you find yourself in that state where it feels really good. Your unconscious mind should know that I'm going to get you to the point where you have orgasm after orgasm after orgasm after orgasm. Multiple ones of those. So that your conscious self gets so flooded with pleasure that it's simply incapable–eight–of doing anything other than feeling good and hearing those numbers. And you can know how you feel. And that's perfectly fine. And you can know how deeply in trance you are. And that's perfectly fine, too. Nine. And at some point in time, your unconscious mind will get to the point where, even without using those numbers–nine–you'll notice that when I say a number, even if I've already said it.

Does it feel like staring inside your own head–nine–there's something about your unconscious mind doing this right now again and again and again which is going to allow it even from some sort of dead, cold, stop, to be able to give your body that experience–ten– of having that orgasm.

[Here, DJ is beginning to pant and whimper audibly.]

The instant I say that phrase. That it's just going to feel so incredibly good, your unconscious mind gets the idea that even without that ramping up it can still make you have that orgasm. From now on, any time it's safe and appropriate, of course, but any time I–and only I–say to you, "DJ, orgasm now."

DJ:    [Groans.]

LA:    You notice that your body just goes through that whole phase, the whole thing. And as we do this more and more and more, you go right back to that 'ten' state, because I want to make sure that your unconscious mind is doing as much of that work as we possibly can. You can go through that whole thing and orgasm now! *Snap!*

DJ:    [Moans.]

LA:    Deeper and deeper and deeper down. More into trance; feel how good it is as you go more deeply into trance, as your unconscious mind makes those superhighways of connections between your brain as I tell that it's ten, and ten, and ten, and ten, and have an orgasm now *Snap!*

DJ:    [More moans.]

LA:    And as your conscious self feels that pleasure and as it hears the sound of my voice you'll know that absolutely nothing else can get in to your conscious mind. That's it. It becomes stuffed with pleasure. It becomes filled with the sound of my voice and the pleasure. And I'm not sure which one is blocking out everything else. Orgasm now! *Snap!*

DJ:    [More groans.]

LA:    But you'll notice that your body just keeps going through these things over and over and over and over again in such a way that it feels really good for you to be right there, in such a way that it feels really good for you to find yourself dropping deeper and deeper, and even more deeply into trance right now. As you feel that pleasure. Orgasm now. *Snap!*

DJ:    [Even more moans.]

LA:    And letting your body get to that place where every single time you have another one—ten...

DJ:    [Shuddering groans now.]

LA:    You notice that it becomes more realistic, more accurate, more exactly the way it is when you have them—ten. And *Snap!* orgasm now. *Snap!*

DJ:    [Heavy breathing and moans.]

LA:    And let's say eleven. *Snap!* Because why not?

DJ:    [Laughs.]

LA: Let your unconscious mind get to that point where even if I turned the radio off, which I'm not, so radio on and ten, so even if I had done that, you'll notice that you can just hear those words from me, with my voice, DJ, orgasm now. *Snap!*

DJ: [Indecipherable pleasurable noises. They do not really stop from this point on.]

LA: Your body simply responds in that way that allows you to simply feel and feel and feel and as you find yourself in that state, let those pleasure waves get stronger and longer. Notice that you can, like women, actually experience a more prolonged feeling of pleasure. Probably more than you expected, but certainly your unconscious mind can make you–orgasm now–feel how good it is to just find yourself in that state. And as you find yourself in that state you'll find you notice that the other things that I share fade away because all my words just go to your unconscious mind, that all the things that I share are with your unconscious self now, simply seem to feel really good. That's all you know. Ten *Snap!* and ten *Snap!* and ten *Snap!* and orgasm now. *Snap!*

And your unconscious mind can just pick up the rest of those words and make them what happens to you. As you find yourself in that state–orgasm now–of dropping down deeper and deeper still–ten, and ten, and ten, and ten–and orgasm now–so that your unconscious mind hears my words and just makes them absolutely happen.

Now, let's find your unconscious self doing something a little different and a little new and a little exciting–orgasm now–because I think this is a good time to introduce some sort of post-hypnotic trigger that your unconscious mind would like to do–orgasm now *Snap!*–and so, let's say that later on today, you're going to find yourself, oh, at say, I don't know, three o'clock your time, you're going to find yourself–orgasm now–kneeling down, to tie your shoe, or whatever, adjust your pant leg, or to do something to your foot. And then at that time, at three o'clock today, you're going to recognize and realize that this is a post-hypnotic suggestion you've been given. And everything can come back to you at that time. Orgasm now. Everything can come back to you, even the things that you've been forgetting. And that's perfectly OK. And when it does come back to you, perhaps then is a good time to add to your notes, or you can send me a little note. Deeper and deeper and deeper down, ten. And ten. And ten. And orgasm now. *Snap!*

DJ: [Some whimpering noises can now be heard.]

LA: And feel so very good right now as you hold on to those things. As you drop. Orgasm now. *Snap!* Deeper and deeper and deeper into trance.

And then, let all of that subside as I count you up from one to ten. Notice that somewhere in the middle the radio will turn itself off and everything will fade away nicely and by the time I'm at nine your conscious self can hear my words. One, two, three, four, five, six, seven, eight, nine and ten. Wide awake.

[There is a pause while DJ collects himself.]

LA: That's a lot of blinking. [Laughs as DJ continues to collect himself and blink.]

DJ: [Laughs.]

LA: [Laughs.] That's still a lot of blinking.

DJ: [Slightly slurring.] Yes. I'm tracking [?.] in and I'm not entirely sure what just happened.

LA: OK? What do you think just happened.

DJ: OK. Well. There're no stains, so that's good.

LA: [Laughs.]

DJ: I feel... um... What? It's for science!

LA: That's right!

[Both laugh.]

LA: Science and scholarly research, dammit!

DJ: ...y-yes!

[More laughing.]

DJ: I've never smoked and I think I need a cigarette.

I feel like I've had a little bit of orgasms [sic]. And that it got very fuzzy and hazy.

LA: OK, I'd say that's about right.

DJ: ...that's all I got.

LA: [Reassuringly.] That's fine.

DJ: How was it on your end?

LA: It's about right. Yeah.

## Notes

DJ: If you had asked me to write something about it before three pm I would have told you that I all I can recollect is some orgasmic feelings and that everything was a bit of a haze. After three pm, I can recall many, many orgasmic peaks, the delightful feeling of being right on the edge at 'ten,' and the strange feeling of 'eleven.'

I am curious to see what Lee thinks of having someone (or me) on a string like that.

Be prepared to feel post-orgasmic afterward (of course) even if 'orgasms' didn't happen. What it felt like to me was as if my body was dumping endorphins into my system over and over again. So the feeling was very erotic, and very pleasurable, but I wasn't having the physical evidence of an orgasm.

LA: I find something fun about using pleasure as a tool. Some humans don't get very much, and this kind of endorphin or oxytocin dump can be beneficial above and beyond causing someone to forget something. There's also something wonderful about seeing someone so relaxed after this kind of event—kind of exhausted, pretty happy, and a lot blissy.

# CHAPTER SIXTEEN

## *Experiment 16 Confusion Overload*

***How do I confuse?***
***Seven Plus or Minus two.***
***Your brain overloads.***

***So many items***
***Tracking all of them is hard***
***You just forget it.***

For some people, this kind of confusion induction totally overwhelms their conscious self and allows them to only focus on one thing, perhaps the sound of your voice, or a feeling of being deep, while all the other things which you might choose to share with them are only registered unconsciously. This induction is based on the idea that our brains can only handle seven pieces of information, plus or minus two, at any given time. So most people can handle five pieces of information, and some can handle up to nine before they begin to lose track of things. This is one reason longer strings of information, like phone numbers, are grouped, which can allow us to remember all ten numbers.

LA:  So. In this one, I don't tell you to go to sleep right away. Which is the fun part of it, isn't it?

DJ:  [Laughs.]

LA:  But the goal of this is that as I mention all of these nine things, and as I go over them, over and over and over again, basically how it works is that our unconscious minds work a little bit like computer processors. But they're computer processors that do one thing at a time. So usually, humans do one thing at a time really, really, well. And especially males tend to do one thing at a time really, really, well. Like, women tend to be a little better at multi-tasking. Men tend to be a little better… I think of men as silos and women as bodies of water. Because women tend to cover a lot more ground, and men are very focused on one little thing, like I've known some men who are very into, say, trains. And they know everything there is to know about a specific kind of car, specific kind of track, what company these cars were manufactured by… whatever. Very detail oriented about one particular thing. Women tend to have a broader area of knowledge that's not always as deep as men's. But it's over many, many, many other things. It's not that men can't have an approach that looks like that, it's that really what they have is a bunch of silos of all sorts of things popping up. So. That's my take on that.*

As you pay attention to the sound of my voice, let your body just notice what temperature your skin feels right now. And as you pay attention to my voice you're also going to notice that there might be other sounds around you, you have a headset on, there may be other sounds that creep through anyway like the sounds of your house. So you can pay attention to the sounds around your house. And the sounds of my voice. And the temperature of the room right now. The feel of the clothing on your body. The way your body feels as it sits on that chair. The way you actually breathe. Maybe you haven't paid attention to your breathing before, but you'll notice that right now you're doing that. So as your mind is doing these things, going around and around and around, from the temperature in the room, to the sounds around you to the feel of your clothing to the sound of my voice to the way you breathe to the way your feet feel on the floor to whatever it is that you're seeing right now. To the way your headphones feel on your head, to the spaces between my words. And as you find yourself focusing on each one of these things in turn, you may notice that your brain begins to sort of go around and around and around as it focuses again on the temperature of the room, the sounds around you, the feel of clothing, the sound of my voice, the way you're breathing, the spaces between my words, the way your feet feel on the floor, and how your headphones feel on your head. And as your unconscious mind thinks about each and every one of those, in fact, as your conscious self thinks about each and every one of those, over and over, faster and faster and faster, the temperature of the room, the sounds around you, the feel of your clothing, the sound of my voice, your breathing, the way your feet feel on the floor, the space between my words, whatever it is you're seeing now and the way that the headphones that you're wearing feel on your head, you'll notice that at some point in time, even as you think about each and every one of those things, in turn, over and over again, at some point in time, your brain decides that it's really receiving a lot of information, and it's really receiving a lot more information than maybe you'd normally think about. More than the temperature in the room, because unless it's perfect, you might find yourself paying attention to it. But otherwise, you don't. But right now, you're paying attention to the temperature in the room, and the sounds that might be around you, the feeling of your clothing, the sound of my voice, your breathing, the way your feet feel on the floor, the spaces between each and every one of my words, whatever it is that you're seeing right now, the way your headphones feel on your head, and maybe what you wore for Halloween last year. So as your conscious mind thinks about each and every one of these things: the temperature in the room, the way the headphones feel on your head, whatever it is you're seeing right now, the sounds around you, the spaces between my words, the feel of your clothing, the sound of my voice, the way you're breathing right now, the way your feet feel on the floor, the way your body feels on that chair, at some point in time your unconscious mind realizes that your conscious self is a little overwhelmed, and overloaded, and before too long, the conscious self just sort of checks out and your unconscious self comes just a little bit closer and a little bit closer, and really for your conscious self it feels so good to just stop thinking about all those things and just find yourself focusing on the one thing that really feels best right now and I don't know what that one thing is. Perhaps you can let that be the sound of my voice. And let everything else simply escape your head. As the sound of my voice fills that, fills that space on any conscious level, so your unconscious mind comes closer and closer and hears my words and your conscious self just hears the sound of my voice, perhaps you've seen or heard a Charlie Brown cartoon, and you know at some point in time that all the adults start talking and when you hear that "wha-wha-whaw" sound, you know that that's the adults talking, and I'm not suggesting that the sound of my voice resembles that by any stretch of the imagination, but you don't actually hear the actual words, your conscious self just focuses on the sounds of my voice, the way it rises and falls, then your unconscious self takes each and every one of my words and those pieces of information, and holds on to them so very tightly and your conscious self just finds itself lulled, by the sound of my voice, flowing through your mind, as your mind becomes blank of anything else, because it feels so good to let your conscious mind go blank, with everything else, except for the sound of my voice, and as your conscious self hears the sound of my voice, and your unconscious self takes all of my words for itself, you might even notice how simple it becomes for your conscious self to think about absolutely nothing other than just that sound.

Now perhaps that sound generates other feelings–I don't know, I'm not sure–but notice how any of those things just pop up and then fade away due to the sound of my voice flowing through your head, like a river. Washing everything away, keeping it new and yet, the same, as though sounds of my voice flow over into your conscious mind, over and over and over again, and you find yourself in this state. Where your unconscious mind simply opens up wider and wider taking my words directly into it, letting my words just simply flow into your mind. So that there's that complete separation, the sound of my voice goes to your conscious self, the words that I'm saying go straight to your unconscious mind and both sides of you become very happy, because you're each receiving a part of what it is that I'm sharing with you, right now. And each of you enjoys and needs the part that it's getting. The sound of my voice doesn't really help your unconscious self much at all, although your unconscious self probably somewhere knows the sound of my voice quite well. And the words that I'm saying right now have no bearing on your conscious self because your conscious self is simply enjoying that space the sound of my voice flowing through it create, while washing everything else out. Notice how good it feels to notice that the only thing your conscious self will hold onto is the sound of my voice. And perhaps any little feelings that popped up. But those will probably be pretty faint. And that's OK. So hold on to what you've held on to, so that you can let me know what that is, or what that isn't. Wide awake on the count of ten. One. Two. Three. Four. Five. Six. Seven. Eight. Nine. Ten. *Snap!* Wide awake!

[Lee laughs as DJ looks around, bleary-eyed.]

LA: Hi.

DJ: Hi.

LA: So how was that?

DJ: [Plaintive sigh.]

LA: [Giggle.]

DJ: That was nice. That felt really deep.

LA: Interesting. So, your eyes were open for quite a bit of that. In the beginning.

DJ: OK.

LA: It looked, sort of early on, like you were not 'there' any more. But I wondered how *you* felt about that.

DJ: I think I am very conditioned to going under for you.

LA: [Giggling.] That might be true.

DJ: I think that is true. It felt like–as you were talking and going through everything–that was entrancing. And it felt like, essentially, was it the other day when you were having me try to do the "Loop," suggestions over and over again, and my brain just was like "Nope, I'm done." It was a little bit of a feeling like that where you're giving me all these things to think about, and I'm ready to give up. I'm ready to go. "Just give the word and I'm out of here." And I think that because one of the things you said was what was I looking at, that's why I was keeping my eyes open. Because I think I wanted to close my eyes. Once it was time to focus on your voice, I was like, "OK, time to go."

LA: Yeah... yeah.

DJ: And I went deep. And I think that's all I remember. So... if there's anything else... I don't remember that.

LA: So, do you remember what the things were that I was talking about? Do you remember all of them? I threw an extra one in there somewhere that I think I just mentioned once, too.

DJ: There was something about Halloween. Which stuck out.

LA: Yes.

DJ: ...I can remember it. But I don't want to remember it.

[Both laugh.]

DJ: It feels like too much work.

LA: Interesting.

DJ: Because... let's see. There was the sound of your voice.

LA: Right.

DJ: And there was whatever I was looking at. [Pause.] Headphones? [Long pause, then laughing.] As I'm going through the list, I'm putting myself into trance.

LA: Excellent! I wondered if that was happening. It kind of looked like it might have been. Because you have to try to remember them, so you're probably going through them. You're like, "Oh... the headphones, this, the voice, what I'm seeing," and then you start to go back into that thing don't you? Yes.

DJ: Yes, I do.

[Both laugh.]

LA: All right.

DJ: (It's so cool.). So, while I probably could theoretically remember, I don't think I could actually say them. Like, if I started at the other end, I could probably work my way back through four of them before I started trancing myself again.

LA: So, for you it only takes four things. I could probably just repeat those four things over and over and over again. And before long you have this little mantra going in your head and you're really not there any more.

DJ: ...yes.

LA: Excellent.

[More evil laughing.]

Just like that.

DJ: Just like that.

## Notes

DJ: Hard to know what to say about this one. Only the fact that one of the items was 'what I was seeing' actually kept my eyes open. I was extremely 'turned on' by the fact that even attempting to remember the items I was given started putting me into a trance. At no point did I think I *couldn't* remember the items. But just trying to was so difficult and opened me up to sending me back down. Highly recommended. (And I'm drifting a little just thinking about it.)

I also think that this, as an induction, is very effective for me because of my general approach towards hypnosis as a surrender of control—by overloading my brain, it makes the surrender to trance as that much more enticing.

LA:   This particular kind of induction can be challenging to demonstrate as often the person you're demonstrating on goes into trance far before you ever get to the seventh thing, let alone the ninth. Keep this in mind when you do this—if your subject goes into trance on the third thing, stop your patter and deliberately put them in trance with whatever their favorite trance words are (the words "Deeper NOW" come to mind for a few of my friends) and then carry on. Some people might like that you keep going because they love inductions, others might just want you to get on with the suggestion part of your interaction. Whatever you do is fine, as long as you're doing it deliberately, and not thinking that you HAVE to go through all nine before you can say, "Deep Sleep!" or whatever it is you prefer.

*Yes, this is a sexist take on how people learn, and of course there are exceptions to the rule, and you gentle readers may know every one of them. I still stand by this as a definite trend/pattern/thing I constantly notice with men and women I know and/or read about. If you're offended, please let it bother you in a way that still allows you to get as much useful information about hypnosis and amnesia out of this book. Also, if you too notice these things to be either true or false for people you know, use that "Silo" or "Shallow and wide" formula to add to the confusion or focus someone has to your and their advantage, perhaps going into excruciating detail for a shallow–and wide–person, and talking about a lot of various things for someone more silo like.

# CHAPTER SEVENTEEN
## *Experiment 17 Freeze and Loop*

***Freeze! Now immobile***
***Eyes and ears turned off as well.***
***No thoughts for this time.***

## FREEZE

Sometimes, as a hypnotist, you just want your subject to do nothing. And sometimes, as a subject, you want the same thing. If part of what draws someone to hypnosis is that feeling of stillness, then the "Freeze" command would give that person everything they'd want, and more.

It's a very simple command, the hypnotist tells the subject to "Freeze." The subject attains a state of physical stillness, and the subject's mind completely blanks out. In short, as far as the subject is concerned, nothing happens in between the time the hypnotist says "Freeze" and gives the "Release" command (or "Unfreeze").

It's a fun trigger and can lead to many instances of the subject not knowing what is happening as people and objects and time itself move around them.

It's also a good trigger for people who want to be 'doing' something, other than sitting and thinking.

Below, find an example of language that Lee has used to implant the trigger in a willing subject, and how we used it.

Freeze and Loop may not seem related, but they are in many ways variations on the same theme.

The "Freeze" trigger is probably one of the most basic hypnotic triggers that one can give to another person. Simply put, the trigger tells the subject to freeze in place and to not be able to move 'no matter what' until the hypnotist gives the counter-trigger. We like to use the word "Release" but any trigger will suffice.

A simple way to achieve this is, once the subject is in trance, use language along these lines:

> "From now on, whenever I–and only I–say 'Freeze!' to you, you immediately stop in place, and your body simply stays that way until I say 'Release!' as long as it's safe and appropriate to do so. No matter how hard you try to move, or whether you try to relax in to a new position, your unconscious simply holds you there, where you were when I said 'Freeze' as comfortably as it's able to. You become as a frozen object, unable to hear (except me saying 'Release') unable to see, unable to move, and content to be, perfectly oblivious to anything around you. Your body temperature remains comfortable as well. Imagine a kind of object which is like that, immobile, staying in place, still, then imagine yourself as still as that object, with similar abilities."

Without amnesia, it can be the source for some good-natured games where the subject is frozen and then, perhaps tickled. One of DJ's first experiences with the trigger was actually at a party where Lee froze DJ and then spent time tickling him, allowing the tickle feeling to build up over time.

Likewise, if one is into more intense BDSM play, a Freeze trigger can serve as a bondage technique, where the subject can be prone to various forms of corporal punishment without being able to react. If this is a direction you are inclined to play in, make sure you reinforce that the trigger can be released so that the subject can use their safe words.

But this use of the trigger allows the subject to remember the events that happen while the trigger is in use. We actually recommend starting with this trigger in this fashion because it works beautifully as a convincer for the more skeptical subject. It's also good clean fun.

Once you have figured out the best way for non-amnesia version of the trigger to work for both of you, go back and, once the subject is in trance, use the following language to adjust the trigger:

> "Once you're in this frozen state, until I wake you up, you become as aware of your surroundings as that object would be, completely oblivious and unaware. Notice that things which happen when you're in that state become things you have no knowledge of, either touch,

sounds, sights, smells, time. When woken up, everything seems as it was just the moment before Freeze was said."

You may be having so much fun that you may ask why you would want to change the trigger.

When combined with an amnesia command, the freeze trigger can truly freeze the subject and there is often an observed difference in the eyes of the subject who is frozen with and without amnesia.

But from the subject's side of things, the difference is palpable. It's as if there is a blank spot in one's mind. There is a fantastic frisson of joy when, seemingly out of nowhere, one's whole world changes around you in the blink of an eye. Using the amnesiac freeze trigger, one can move items or people around the room, or change a person's clothes. If one seeks a more 'hardcore' BDSM experience, one could even freeze the subject, tie them down or bind them with rope, and then release them from the trigger. Fans of tease and denial can freeze their subject just before an orgasm. There are any number of games one can play.

LA:  DJ, deep sleep, all the way down. And since it's been so long, I'm going to remind your unconscious self that I'd like you to go to that place that your unconscious self knows that your conscious self is in that place where it simply pays zero attention where my words go, directly to your unconscious mind, and so you find you have both amnesia for this session, and as I install both loop and freeze you can find yourself in that place you find yourself in that place where because you've forgotten even though you knew what we were going to do today because you've forgotten that session you'll find that they both work so much better.

So this is how "Freeze" goes: any time I–and only I–say "DJ, freeze," or maybe just "Freeze," and my intent is that—I'm not talking the freezer or something cold, I'm talking about you stopping in place. You'll find yourself automatically stopped in place. It's more than just finding yourself stopped in place unable to move, you find yourself completely unaware of whatever is going on around you. Unconsciously you'll be able to hear my voice saying "Release," or I might say "Unfreeze" or whatever. Again, as long as you understand that my intent is for to let you go. (If I said to you "Melt" I wonder what "Melt" would do to you?) Let's just go with "Unfreeze" or "Release" for right now.

What happens to you in that state? Your body is at normal temperature. But between the "Freeze" which you may or may not consciously be aware of, and the "Release," which again you may or may not consciously be aware of, it appears there have been zero moments in between. So you go from one to the other just this quickly, *Snap!* no matter how much time has passed.

No matter where you happen to be, no matter where other people happen to be, it's as though you blinked and suddenly, *Snap!* something different happened. And whatever happened in between, you don't know what that is. Because it was just a *Snap!* blink to you. Does that make sense to your unconscious mind? Is that clearer than we talked about it before?

[DJ reaches up and touches his chin in response to both questions.]

LA: Is there anything else, that we could do that would make it more clear, more useful, more amnesiac for DJ that you can think of?

[DJ shakes his head no.]

[After bringing DJ up from the trance.]

LA: I was going to say, do you have a headache now?

So, DJ, freeze. Just like that. I don't know what happens with your eyes open. Your unconscious may decide it makes no difference with your eyes open or closed, in terms of how well it responds. And of course, it may make a huge difference. [While Lee is talking, she is moving her computer around the room so there is an entirely different background.] Release.

DJ: Huh. That's a nice little jump.

LA: I wonder just how–Pause!–Freeze! [Lee moves again.] Here, I'll show you the outside. Release.

DJ: [Laughs.]

LA: That's my front yard.

DJ: It's a nice yard.

LA: Well we're seeing it from the second floor. Let's see. Loop!

[DJ sits quietly, while Lee moves about her office again.] I wonder if we'll have the same effects. [After 30 seconds, DJ 'comes to.']

LA: So, what were those effects?

DJ: This is so much fun. What was your question?

LA: What were those effects?

DJ:   Of what?

LA:   What you just did.

DJ:   What…?

LA:   Well, you said this is so much fun. What was fun?

DJ:   Well, just how you moved around. One moment you were in one place, and the next you were somewhere else.

LA:   No. I invented teleportation, it's really awesome.

DJ:   Yes. [Sarcastically.] You invented teleportation. I believe everything you say. You great goddess.

LA:   You know all my life, I've wanted to be in one place, instantaneously and that hasn't happened, I blame Star Trek. Those damn supermarket people got those doors open like magic. So why isn't teleportation the next logical step. Isn't that something Spock would say? We've got that figured out, why not teleportation?

DJ:   If only Spock were real.

LA:   Yeah, yeah, yeah. So I think those two are definitely working better.

DJ:   … Did we do two different ones?

LA:   Yes.

DJ:   … OK great!

LA:   We definitely did the two I said we were going to do today, which I will not name, because… you know. Because, you'd forget. And it'd be awkward.

DJ:   Right. 'Cause you hate awkward things like that.

LA:   Yeah. I do. And I don't have anything to drink. Well, I do. But it's all the way over there.

DJ:   Well. Just teleport over there.

LA:   Yeah. Freeze. [Lee gets up and goes over to her drink. Picks it up. Walks back to her chair.] And release. Better yet, I teleported it over to me.

DJ:   [Laughs.]

# LOOP

***Skip back in your time***
***And replay what just happened;***
***Nothing new will stick.***

The "Loop" trigger is, in sense, an outgrowth of the "Freeze" trigger, and can be, in many ways, more immediately entertaining for the hypnotist. In this trigger, the subject finds themself reliving the last 30 seconds or so. This usually takes the form of the subject repeating everything that they have said, in the same manner that they did the first time. One way to describe the trigger to the subject is as follows:

> "From now on whenever I–and only I–say to you 'DJ, Loop!,' you automatically and easily take the last five seconds of your conversations and your actions and do them over and over and over again for 30 seconds.

> Can your unconscious handle that? Excellent. And what happens while you are in that loop state, what you remember, is what you've done. But you remember that you've done it once as opposed to six times. You remember that you've done it once and everything else that has happened around you during that time is unimportant. There might have been something that happened during one of those times that you did it, but the only time that you remember—I don't know if it's the first time or the last time, is only one of those times. You might remember other people doing other things at the same time of that five second period you remember, but otherwise, during that time, other stuff can go on and your brain just lets it go as though it never saw it or heard it, felt it or any of those things. OK? OK."

From the outside, the person seems caught in a loop for those 30 seconds. Internally, the subject will not notice any time passing—they will probably only experience the first five of those 30 seconds. The subject will come to experience it much like the "Freeze" trigger, with the feeling that nothing has happened for the period of time that they were 'stuck in a loop' even as the world changes around them in that period of time.

The trigger can be altered so that it can be given "Loop, three times," and the subject will relive those 30 seconds three times in a row. Alternatively, the instruction can be given so that the hypnotist can say "Loop for two minutes, five times" and the subject will loop the last two minutes of their life five times.

Certain subjects should probably be reassured that exactitude is not necessary. However, Lee has found that when she uses the "Loop" trigger on many of her more practiced subjects in mid-conversation, they repeat the last few seconds or minutes of their conversation verbatim.

With the subject's permission, making an audio recording of the "Loop" can result in a very fantastic convincer and proof that the subject is both experiencing amnesia and a very good subject.

In any event, there are many ways to play with both the "Freeze" and "Loop" triggers, and we hope you find it as fun to play with as we have.

### Notes on Freeze

DJ:    This seemed to work quite well. It's hard to know what happened in the interim while I was "Frozen." It did seem very much like Lee 'teleported' since she changed position from one part to another. This one seemed like an unqualified success.

# CHAPTER EIGHTEEN

## *Experiment 18 Forgetting Orgasm Trigger*

**Who would ever think
Coming over and over
Would be a mindfuck?**

In the movie *Matrix: Reloaded*, a character called "The Merovingian" has a monologue about causality. As part of the monologue, he causes a chocolate desert to be given to a person in a restaurant. He has 'programmed' the desert to 'force' the person to have an orgasm. The person has the uncontrollable orgasm and excuses herself to leave the dining room.

This scene lingered with Lee, and she used it as inspiration. For her, instead of using chocolate cake (because there is a limited amount of chocolate cake available) she used water, which is both readily available and healthy. Since then, Lee and DJ have had a lot of fun with this trigger, and DJ has been extremely well-hydrated.

LA: So now we should do number 18. This is one of the things that's on my Big Trigger list, so this is not one of my suggestions. I've got a few of my own suggestions in the Big Trigger list, but this is somebody else's. It's a take off of something from *The Matrix*. It's called the "Merovingian."

DJ: Oh, yes.

LA: Basically where you have an orgasm… now, in the movie, the way I've read it before, you decide that you want a bite of something and the instant you take a bite of it you have an orgasm. But the act of having the orgasm, when its over, makes you forget that you've had it, but also makes you really, really, really want more of whatever actually caused it. And so it's this whole, you know, I don't really want a bite of that, but, um, you know. I'll eat it because… and then I've forgotten I know it does this thing.

I would say that every time you have one it should get more powerful. Until by the end, you know your body is getting better at both having orgasms without you knowing and creating that desire to have more. But you probably don't have cake in front of you, and you may not be interested in cake anyway.

DJ: No. I'm interested in cake. Or bisque* for that matter.

LA: Yeah, that bisque was really good.

DJ: It was very good.

[Both laugh.]

DJ: Here's the thing… you're going to laugh.

LA: OK.

DJ: What flavor was the bisque?

LA: Butternut squash.

DJ: OK. Thank you.

LA: Why?

DJ: I couldn't remember.

LA: [Laughs.] I am laughing. That's funny.

DJ: See?

LA: It was butternut squash and it was good butternut squash. I mean, I think butternut squash is delightful anyway, but that bisque was really, really, delicious. You know, and it's so simple. Like who would have thought that you take one of these gourds and you chop it up and you add some onions and some salt and pepper and butter and cream and viola! Heaven on a plate… or a bowl, or whatever. It was so thick it almost could have been on a plate. But anyway. So good. All right. So…?

Deep sleep! *Snap!*

Just all the way down, down, down, down, down, down, down, down, more and more and more. Just about to where you were last time. And you can include some of that pleasure too. And we can do what we were doing before, where you find yourself in that state where you hear the sound of my voice, consciously, and you feel all that pleasure, consciously. And

116

unconsciously... well, your unconscious mind can experience as much pleasure as it would like, there's really no restrictions for your unconscious self right there. And that's perfectly fine. Perfectly fine.

In the meantime, let's give you a couple of suggestions. So, "Radio on," and ten. *Snap!* All the way, right there.

DJ:   [Grunts, slightly.]

LA:   Deeper and deeper and deeper down. And as you find yourself sinking more deeply into that trance state where you feel so good–Ten–where your conscious self feels that pleasure–Ten–orgasm now.

DJ:   [Makes similar sounds as before.]

LA:   And you find yourself in that state where you feel the pleasure and you hear the sound of my voice in your conscious self then go ahead, and go ahead, and go ahead again.

DJ:   [Some moans.]

LA:   Let your unconscious self just take up these words. Just for today, when you find yourself coming wide awake when I tell you to in the future, notice that you really, really, really are thirsty, and you want a sip of your water or whatever happens to be in your thermos, and as you find yourself in that state where you want a little bit to drink, you'll notice that every single time you do it, you take a drink and you have an orgasm, and then you completely and absolutely forget all about it, except that you find yourself becoming thirsty, again and again and again, and you may notice that you find yourself having a stronger response–Orgasm Now–*Snap!* every single time you have another orgasm, after you've taken that sip. Notice how powerful it is. Of course, protect your teeth, and your body. But you'll notice how simple it becomes for you to forget that you've had an orgasm and yet to want to have another one and to take a sip and have another one and not realize that the water, and whatever happens to be in there is actually causing that. So as your unconscious mind gets a little bit of that, how you're going to find yourself compelled to drink some water, and how taking that drink makes you have an orgasm and how immediately after it, you forget it, except what it does create is a desire for more water, or more of whatever you're drinking. So as your unconscious mind goes "Yep, yep, yep, I'll make that allll happen," just go ahead and lift your hand up and tell me "Yes." All the way to your chin.

[DJ does this.]

And then, wide awake… right now. *Snap!*

[The following discussion is included as an example of this trigger working very well. Please note all the times DJ takes a drink of water, his responses to it, and his responses as we talk about doing something we've JUST done.]

DJ:  [Glares.]

LA:  [Laughing.] What's that for?

DJ:  [Audible sigh.] Just, you know, a puppet on a string. Enjoying it.

LA:  [Makes reference to a horrible DirecTV commercial, where this woman walks in who has been made into a puppet, a literal puppet.]

DJ:  [Takes a drink of water. The recording catches a moan.]

LA:  [Laughs.]

DJ:  [Again, another drink. Another moan.]

LA:  So, I think that, we'll probably—

DJ:  [Yet another drink and moan.]

LA:  We can probably get through some of the others. Like the others are more

DJ:  [Another drink and groan.]

LA:  sort of…

DJ:  [The sound of gasping.]

LA:  No, no… we should definitely do a couple of the other ones. Not all of them, maybe. Mmm. Yeah.

DJ:  What—what else is on the list.

LA:  OK. So, "19" is count backwards by threes.

DJ:  Oh. Right.

LA:  Say something out loud/having a mantra.

DJ:  Right.

LA: Um. Dual inductions and multiple-tracks and audios. The fade away. So for the first five minutes you remember everything perfectly clearly and then after that nothing. Unless I specifically bring it up within the next day or so, it just disappears, leaving you only with the feelings of how good or deep or exciting the trance was. The Esdaile State. The forget switch on. The fractionation, partially up then deepener. I'm not sure about that one, I think that that one will be very, very effective—

DJ: [There has been more sounds of gasping as Lee was talking just now, but here the gasps become much more audible.]

LA: —as a technique that's useful for amnesia.

DJ: I'm sorry… which one?

LA: Number 25, the fractionation, partially up then deeper. And I think it's because if you allow someone to go into a very deep state of trance they sometimes just don't remember what happened anyway, and they start to wake up with that "What the hell just happened?" or "Did something just happen?" kind of feeling.

DJ: I think I know what that feeling is like.

LA: [Laughs.] Yeah.

DJ: [Gasps.] There's a post-hypnotic suggestion going on right now, isn't there?

LA: Um… There is…

DJ: OK.

LA: Why?

DJ: Just checking.

LA: Yes. It's less a post-hypnotic suggestion, although it clearly is—

DJ: [Gasps.]

LA: than a demonstration of number 18.

DJ: [Reads through the list of experiments. Hits number 18. Starts laughing.] That just seems mean.

LA: Because you're forgetting the orgasm??

DJ: Yes!

LA: I see. Wellllll. [Laughs.] Would it be more helpful if it was ice water?

DJ: Why?

LA: Because you could just put it on your forehead.

DJ: Why… oh… I see.

LA: So wait, what do you see?

DJ: [Sighs.] What–what do you mean?

LA: You just said "Oh, I see." I'm trying to figure out what your understanding is of what's going on right here, right now.

DJ: Wow. My subconscious is hiding something from me. And is doing it rather actively.

LA: Really? What a nice subconscious mind you have.

DJ: [Sarcastic laughter.] Oh. You know… [Drinks. Gasps.] I like to play along.

LA: [Laughs. Drinks her own water.]

DJ: [Pauses.]

LA: Yeah. I don't want to do this for much longer because sometimes you're actually looking at me, and I want to make sure that you're not-like– stopping in the middle of something. And other times, I don't actually care. [Drinks.]

DJ: [Pauses.] Then laughs. [Drinks. Then moans.] I'm glad I turned out to be a good subject.

LA: Yes! I bet you are. I mean, I didn't think you were a bad subject to begin with, but I definitely saw some signs that you were [DJ moans.] getting better at that.

LA: I definitely think we should do "Forget switch on." I mean, I like using the control room as a technique. And I like the idea that—yes?

DJ: I can't believe I've downed most of this bottle of water.

LA: Why?

DJ: I didn't think I was that thirsty.

LA:  I see.

DJ:  [Drinks. Gasps. Crumples bottle.]

LA:  [Nonchalantly.] Um. I did send you the thing on going through the door. And I'd like to do that again.

DJ:  OK.

LA:  And then the implanted memories. Oh! So. I saw this thing on taking bad memories and making them better. Basically it talks about how you take your bad memories—now, I don't really have a ton of bad memories, and even the ones that are 'bad' I look back and think, "Yeah, I was an idiot, whatever. Let's move on." There are a lot of people who have terrible memories and they say to focus on, like, something like a friend you were with or what you were wearing, or something else other than what actually happened, and that it alleviates some of the, I guess the pain of it being a bad memory. Which I think is really kind of fascinating. All right, so. I think there are a couple of things that are really similar and I want to group them all together. So the counting backwards by three, then saying something out loud… There's another one or two.

Yes? Why are you threatening me with your empty water bottle from 3,000 miles away? [Laughs.]

DJ:  Oh. No reason… None whatsoever. [Big sigh.]

LA:  Have your conscious self concentrate on other things. I think all of those are related in technique, in having your conscious self focus on something. I think the overload kind of does that too.

DJ:  Sort of like distraction techniques.

LA:  Yeah.

DJ:  Makes sense.

LA:  And so if you're focused on something, then you're not focused on anything else I'm doing. And that's OK by me. It's not that I *never* want people to know what I'm up to. It's just that, most of the time, you really don't need to know. And it'll be good for you.

DJ:  [Laughs.]

LA: So there. So why don't we do 19 and 20 later, and let's add 24. I want to make sure we do the Esdaile state last. Even if we end up doing everything else until that one.

The following transcript is from the next day:

LA: So your wife said that the forgetting about the orgasm thing was "dastardly."

DJ: Ah… yes. Particularly the remembering it a few hours later. Because she came home ten minutes after three.

LA: And you were in a state of "Oh my god, what have I done?"

DJ: "Goodness gracious. I don't know what just happened." She said that I was still kind of woozy when I greeted her, and she said "Wow, your face is really red right now." I said, "I am not surprised, and I don't have a whole lot of ideas about what just happened."

LA: [Laughs.] And now you do.

DJ: And now I do. It was pretty damn cool.

LA: Yeah. I think that's a lot of fun. And again, I think your brain did an excellent job of shutting that out. Like, you knew something had happened, but you didn't know what had happened.

DJ: Oh. I figured it out.

LA: Oh, you did? Well, we had talked about it, so we knew what was going to happen.

DJ: Well, I knew it was going to happen. And, at some point, because, I was looking at the list and the "Merovingian" was there, and I was holding the water in my hand, and wondering why I was drinking so much water. And I thought, "Oh…This is causing me orgasms that I'm forgetting." And just as I was about to say that, my subconscious was like, "Yeah, but it's more fun if we don't."

LA: [Laughs.]

DJ: "So, have a drink."

LA: [Laughs.]

DJ: "And let's distract you, and think about something else."

LA: It did an excellent job of that, by the way.

DJ: Thank you. So, once three o'clock rolled around, and I went to tie my shoes that didn't need tying, and it all came back. I was saying "Oh... Oh!? Oh... Oh!"

LA: [Laughs.]

DJ: So it was a lot of revelations, which was great fun. And, particularly for someone like me, I think where it's important for me to hold on to certain memories of things, it was important to have that permission to later on remember everything; it really helped.

LA: That's just what I was going to say. I think that made a big difference in the way your unconscious mind went "Oh, yes. This is fine." That's one of the things that I noticed with the people that I was doing regular hypnosis sessions with, and doing amnesia stuff, that, at some point in time they would remember. And the whole remembering of that–it wasn't necessarily a big deal–but they kind of wanted to forget, they kind of wanted to not know what was going on. And so creating more and more barriers over time became something that was really important in a process. Because, if you layer a lot of these things together, like if you send your conscious self away, and you only give it one thing to think about, and you build a space between your conscious and your unconscious, and you give you unconscious information and it promises in its own big or little way, to hold on to something and to not share it... and that's difficult because one of my subjects says that his unconscious is like a six-year-old with a secret. So you can do those things and that's a whole bunch of stuff going on. So you might get flashes of something, but you won't really be able to hold on to it well. And then if you take something like, say, "Every time you get closer to remembering what it is, it just fades away," or you find yourself distracted by something else. It's just one more layer and one more layer and one more suggestion, and all of those things can really add to that experience of having that amnesia.

So, of course, the three o'clock, and the shoe, were suggestions in and of themselves. Your brain is clearly very good at following along with that; it didn't know that it was going to do that. But there it was at three o'clock doing that thing.

DJ: I knew there was something I was supposed to do at three o'clock.

LA: OK. You did.

DJ: That was the only thing that stuck with me; I kept on looking at the clock, and thinking, OK, so, three o'clock is coming up.

LA: But you didn't know what it was?

DJ: I'm supposed to do something at three o'clock. And that's as much as I think I remember.

LA: And I don't know if I told you to not remember those, or not. I'm not sure. We could go back through the audio. But I don't remember off the top of my head.

So there's that.

But I really like that idea of forgetting that someone's had an orgasm. I think it's kind of fun.

## Notes

DJ: That water sure was tasty. Looking back on it, it feels like I was just playing along, since all the memories are there in a row. But at the time, I knew that I was 'hiding' the orgasms from myself, even when I pieced together what was happening. It felt like I blasted the revelation from my mind so I could keep going. For both this and the previous experiment, I think that knowing that I would remember eventually was very helpful to my mind accepting the temporary amnesia.

LA: While it may be dastardly to make someone forget orgasms they've had, this method is also very fun. On that order, we have another way we do this that has proved exciting, companionable and occasionally competitive! If you've ever seen the television show "Doctor Who," you may know of a 'monster' called "The Silence," a fictional religious order who resemble the figure from "The Scream" by Edvard Munch.

In the program, the existence of the Silence is a secret because anyone who looks at them immediately forgets that they've seen them once they look away. However, any suggestions the Silence have given them are retained, and they've been able to be a 'pervasive influence' across human history while being difficult to locate or resist. (1) https://en.wikipedia.org/wiki/Silence_%28Doctor_Who%29

One way the heroes in the program have kept track of when they've seen the Silence is by making a hash mark on their hand, using a pen, to count the number of times they've been in contact. There are some terrifying scenes of people with these hash marks all over their bodies.

We have used the concept of the Silence and these hash marks in our play to great effect. The way we do this is I generally 'seed' a few marks on

DJ's arm, which he promptly forgets about. At a later point, I ask him what's on his arm. When he sees the marks, he has one orgasm for each mark (or if there are lots, I may allow him to have one orgasm for each batch or just one in total) which he forgets about after experiencing, adds in one more mark on his arm, which he also forgets about, and carries on. We have several variations on marks on the arm at this point, but the premise is the same.

We did this at DMDW (DeepMindDarkWood) in 2014. When other people saw what was going on, they gave the suggestion to their subjects. At some point in the weekend, there was a friendly competition to see who could have the most orgasms (or give to others who were playing), and a friendly goodbye hug (with marked arms outstretched toward the other person) turned into so much more.

DJ and I have worked it out so that he will remember his orgasms later that day or after the weekend. Once, I had him 'store' the orgasms for later use. When I had him experience the 200 or so orgasms all at once, he collapsed to the floor. (If you do this with your subject, make sure there are no breakable objects nearby.)

It is a lot of fun to watch or experience, and it also serves as a fantastic positive reinforcement for the amnesia: the pleasure of orgasm and the experience of amnesia become closely linked. The subject may soon find that they crave the amnesia because of the reward. This is one of the many ways DJ's facility with amnesia–already good to begin with–became more and more encouraged and entrenched.

* The bisque reference was in regard to a meal at NEEHU 5, where the butternut squash bisque was one of the very best things most of us at the table ate.

# CHAPTER NINETEEN

## *Experiment 19 The Collaborative Countdown*

### *Counting down backwards*
### *It can be tedious work,*
### *Sends you very deep*

Sometimes, one can use the hypnotic induction itself as a means of achieving hypnotic amnesia. This can be a very powerful tool, because it means that the mind is in an amnesiac state from the very beginning. One of the more effective inductions we've found involves giving the conscious mind something to work at while the hypnotist is giving the subject commands. Essentially, the subject is having the conscious mind engage in something tricky, while the unconscious mind is attended to.

Here, DJ was asked to count backwards from 1,000 by threes, while Lee talked to him. This may seem like an oddly specific request, but it's a number that makes sense. It's not actually divisible by three, and it's a large enough number that the hypnotist has time to perform whatever inductions are necessary. And it's small enough that it appears to the subject to be achievable.

The subject is asked to count by threes backwards because it is a task that most people simply don't have experience doing. It gives the conscious mind something to grapple with. It's not rote, but it's also not impossible.

For people who are more mathematically inclined, however, Lee has asked those subjects to say the alphabet backwards, or, perhaps, spell the 50 states backwards.

As we will see, DJ was pleasantly surprised by how well this method worked, not only as a means for amnesia, but as a means of going very, very, deep.

LA:   I'm going to talk with you, and you'll listen to me in addition to counting backwards by threes. If you're a super math person, we should talk about that action, because 'super math people' probably could do that easily, and it wouldn't be as distracting for them. Likewise, perhaps for someone who's really fabulous in English, if we gave them something that they memorized, that they knew and told them to, you know, go backwards every third word from the end. And see how well they'd find themselves remembering that. Would that be all that they could focus on because they knew it so well? Would they additionally be able to pay attention to anything else that was being said to them? I don't have an answer for that either. I don't know. But counting backwards by threes is really easy as a distraction because I think there are fewer people who are really math literate. Although we know quite a few. I know two math teachers, at least. They could probably do some of those without any issues at all.

We were sort of talking about a math confusion induction. If you're really getting someone in a state of, "Here's this problem and I'd like you to work on it in your mind," maybe their conscious self goes, "Oh! Dum-dee-dum-da-da-da," and starts writing it out like using chalk on a board. And maybe that's all they could remember, because they get so into it. That's the same as focusing someone's mind on something.

DJ:   Would a similar thing be "I'll say the alphabet backwards but for every letter come up with a word that beings with that letter and when I hit 'A' come back around and start over at 'Z,' and come up with a different word the second time, and a third time," and so forth? So you're essentially trying to get them to concentrate on something else as well as using some of the creative aspects of it.

LA:   That could be an interesting thing, and then have them remember the things that they said. Or what if they could only remember nine of the words that they could come up with? All for different letters. So that could be an interesting way to focus elsewhere.

DJ:   So should we try the numbers thing, or should we just write this off as a coordination day?

LA:   No we should definitely do this today.

So, what I'd like you to do is to start with a thousand. Count backwards out loud from a thousand by threes. And as you find yourself doing that and saying those words, I'm going to talk to you, and we'll just see what happens. But what's really going to happen. [DJ takes a drink and has a hypnotic orgasm.] You can take a drink. That's fine. [Laughs.] You cannot hide behind the water bottle.

DJ:     Yes. That's perhaps the least effective way of hiding ever.

LA:     [Laughs.] It is now.

DJ:     [Laughs sarcastically.]

LA:     Yes. So, as you begin counting now...

[Throughout the following, DJ can be heard counting backwards from one thousand by threes.]

...I'm just going to keep talking. And as you find yourself doing that, you'll notice that with every number that gets lower than the number before, you find yourself sliding into a trance state. Now you'll find it as easy to keep doing the numbers as your brain finds it easy to do that math. Just subtracting three from the number before it and knowing how easy it is to find yourself staying on track. But as you say those numbers out loud, your unconscious mind pays attention to my voice. And your conscious self really needs to stay alert to what it's doing in order to figure out those things. So your conscious self can pay attention to the counting and to the numbers and the sound of my voice and really, you can just let all those lovely words just slide right on past it over to your unconscious mind. And as your unconscious mind is paying complete and total attention to my voice, you'll notice how simple it is for you to find yourself deeply, deeply, deeply in trance. Deeply in that state where you are aware of what you are doing and pretty much completely unaware of whatever I am doing on any sort of a conscious level. You know you're going into trance, you know you're saying those numbers out loud. Your eyes can be open or shut, it doesn't matter. But what is important is that your unconscious mind is picking up my words. Letting them slide into your unconscious mind, knowing that your conscious self is so occupied with everything else that you are doing. And as your unconscious mind is paying attention to my words and holding on to them very tightly, let's just do one thing.

Let's add in that trigger from before. The Merovingian. (This is an orgasm trigger.) And notice that your conscious self can simply let go of any of that. You can remember it as our conversation that we had earlier. And then any other attempts at remembering that simply fly out the window. Deeper and deeper down, right now. As you keep saying those numbers effortlessly and easily.

And then as you give in to how good it feels to be pulled deeper and deeper by those numbers, notice that your unconscious mind simply becomes a little bit better and a little bit better and a little bit better at ensuring that my words go straight to your unconscious. Really easily and effortlessly go straight to your unconscious mind. And maybe your unconscious self can share with your conscious self that I've been saying these numbers with you all along. So that as you say these numbers all that your conscious self thinks about is that I'm actually counting along with you.

DJ:    859… 856…

    DJ & LA [in unison]: 853… 850… 847… 844… 841…

    [DJ continues.]

LA:    And you'll know as your unconscious mind takes my words, that part of you will remember just hearing my voice saying numbers with you, as you slide down more deeply and especially when you find yourself coming up out of trance. That's what your unconscious mind will let your conscious self hold on to. That I've been saying those numbers with you the whole entire time. Think about how good it feels to know that I've been saying those numbers with you the whole entire time. So how could I possibly have said anything else to you?

DJ:    … 820… 817…

LA:    That's right.

    DJ & LA [in unison]:  814…811…808… 805…

LA:    And as you find yourself heading into the 700s, by the time you get there notice that you're wide awake again.

DJ:    … 799… 796… [wakes up]… Wow!… Ooof.

LA:    So what's the 'wow' about that?

DJ:    I'm still coming up. I felt really deep.

LA:    You can come up on one, two, three, four, five wide awake!

DJ:    Thanks.

LA:    You're welcome.

DJ: I think you saying them with me was really effective. That was pretty awesome.

LA: Yeah?

DJ: That was... wow. Yeah. That was very good. Because it really felt... I think my conscious mind started focusing on that. Which is really difficult, because math isn't that easy for me, because you're starting with a number that isn't divisible by three. So it was a relief when I hit 970 because it meant I was still on track because it was 30 off of a thousand. I thought, "Good, I haven't skipped anything."

LA: [Laughs.]

DJ: Yeah. So I went really deep.

LA: Pretty quickly, too, because, you got a few hundred numbers down, essentially... so you actually counted about a hundred numbers.

DJ: I did?

LA: And the fact that you could get that deep counting basically from 100 down to one, essentially, but in a way that was much more challenging is kind of fun. And how much information got put into your head during that time is also fun for me!

DJ: Yeah. That's the question. I have a memory of you counting with me. So if you're counting with me...? Were you counting with me?

LA: Yes.

DJ: [Uncertainly.] OK. So, what sort of thing did you do, then?

LA: [Laughs.] I did all sorts of things.

DJ: [Laughs.]

LA: Do you really want to know?

DJ: Well... I assume I'll find out one day.

LA: "For science!'

DJ: [Laughs.] You may enjoy the experience of having me not remember what it was.

LA: Oh, well. I only counted with you some of the time. But I made you think that I was counting with you the whole time.

DJ: Nice! Oh, wow!

LA: I re-implanted that other trigger that you seem to enjoy so much the other day. [Starts laughing.] So you can keep enjoying [that drink] or I could take it away right now. It's your choice.

[Both laugh.]

LA: Oh. Just one more sip.

DJ: You tease.

LA: I was thirsty.

[Both laugh some more.]

DJ: OK, now.

LA: So, is it more effective to have a forgetful suggestion, in a forgetful session?

DJ: [Drifts a little, laughs.]

LA: I'm not sure. It could be.

DJ: It's tricky, because on one level I can feel myself remembering everything. But there's another level in which I'm like, "No! No! It's more fun this way."

LA: So what do we do to strengthen that level that goes "No, it's more fun that way?" That sort of immediately shuts down that other level that goes "I remember." Maybe we need to put the level that says, "No, it's more fun this way," over and above the level that says, "No…don't I remember a little bit?". And this part never gets this information. This part is just having a good time enjoying it.

DJ: There're a couple things that I think are at play here. One is the part of me that wants to play along because we're working on a book here.

LA: [Drinks water.]

DJ: [Freezes.] …I love how effective that is.

LA: Me too!

DJ: That's part of it, I mean, even though we're recording this—for posterity— There's still part of my brain that, because we're working on a book on it, the analytical part of my brain is thinking, "I need to hold on to this because I need to remember"–ironically–"what the experience of forgetting is so I can write about that."

LA: And, I think that when we're finished with this, up to the point of time when we start to work on something new, that involves amnesia, that we can just have that whole experience continue for you. When we begin working on new things, you can remember them in their entirety. You certainly need to remember some of the things that we're doing now, for this. Because you've had this experience of "What is my brain doing...?"

DJ: [Had taken a drink of water.] Is it still working?

LA: I think so, I think so. Because you've been clutching that bottle of water.

DJ: [Laughs.] I don't know what you're talking about.

LA: Like you're *really* enjoying it or something.

DJ: [Takes a drink, a gasping sigh is heard.]

LA: [Laughing.] Yep. It's still on.

[Both laugh.]

DJ: So for the purposes of this, I think some reinforcement would work for me–and this is just me speaking for myself and not for other people–is reinforcing both that I'm going to remember it later, that this is for my enjoyment.

LA: Yes.

DJ: That it'll be "More fun this way." It would also be helpful, I'm thinking, and I'm wondering how this dynamic might work for other people, that it's for *your* enjoyment, too. That you get a lot of enjoyment out of it. Because the bottom/submissive part of me wants to make you happy in these sessions.

LA: Yes.

DJ: That extra reinforcement of, "This is going to make you really happy to do this because the loss of control, for whatever reason." Providing this service of going under and saying "Yes, I'm getting something out of this."

But it's also something that you're getting something out of, for whatever reason, like—

LA: Just because I'm devious like that.

DJ: Right. Because, speaking as a subject and someone with a submissive streak, you want to make your top proud of you, happy with you, whatever it is to make the subject secure by reinforcing those things.

LA: It's interesting because for me, I want to also know that your brain is learning new skills. And I know that this is actually a skill that your brain actually can have. So you can improve your memory as a skill. And you can learn to do other things, unconsciously moving your body or talking or whatever-ing while you're deeply in trance, as a skill, and this particular aspect of forgetting is also a skill. I think it's important to recognize that our brains do all sorts of fascinating things, and the more we can teach our brains to do, the more we consciously realize we're capable of doing, and who knows what that might get us to someday? And I think those are big deals.

So I think that was kind of fun. We didn't do that with letters, but maybe we can do that with letters another time.

[DJ drinks water, sighs.]

### Notes

DJ: This was a stunningly effective induction. I think giving my conscious self something to actively 'do' while Lee sent me into a trance really helped both achieving a deep trance as well as facilitating my lack of memory of what else was or wasn't happening. It was easily the deepest I can remember going under any scenario

# CHAPTER TWENTY

## *Experiment 20 Mantras*

**What's one good mantra?**
**"I am a mindless trance slut."**
**Works well for our friend.**

**Repeating these words**
**Consumes all your attention**
**"I simply forget"**

Another way of 'distracting' the conscious mind, or engaging it in some behavior while work is done with the unconscious mind, is to give the conscious mind a mantra. This is often used in hypno-dominations scenarios, where the mantra can be a reinforcement of submissive feelings.

Often, phrases like, "Obedience is pleasure," or "Giving in brings me joy,' can be used. But other phrases without the patina of dominance and submission can be used. For example, "The deeper I go, the better I feel; the better I feel, the deeper I go." A good mantra is one that is has some kind of rhythm to it, is easy to say, and conveys some kind of message.

Some of Lee's audios (available at www.leeallure.com) contain mantras for the listener to repeat as the audio (and her inductions and suggestions) continues. As with "Counting Backwards," engaging the conscious mind can often lead to opening up the unconscious mind. It's as if the conscious mind's propensity for guarding the self takes a holiday.

Here, DJ had listened to one of Lee's audios recently that contained the mantra "Obeying Lee is Blissful Pleasure." This is the mantra DJ settled on as the session went on. Nearly any other appropriate mantra would probably have worked. As with the Countdown, DJ found the method extremely effective, as we'll see.

LA:  [Giggle.] Deep sleep! *Snap!*

Down deeper and deeper and deeper and deeper. So I'm going to let you pick a mantra. I don't know what it's going to be. Notice that it can be three to ten words, somewhere in there. And your brain just picks it and then just begins to say it out loud. And as your brain picks it and begins to say it out loud, notice that as you say it out loud, what happens is that the sound of your own voice begins to drown out the sound of my own voice. No matter what it is that you say, you find yourself in the state of picking that mantra, of saying that phrase out loud, and finding yourself going more deeply into trance. And that becomes the thing you find yourself thinking about and saying and feeling and doing.

[DJ can be heard softly repeating the phrase "Obeying Lee is blissful pleasure.".]

In fact, that phrase that you're saying right now can become the only thing you hear, no matter how loudly or quietly you're talking, your brain knows the sound of your own voice, and your brain knows how you talk, and your brain can become highly, highly, attuned to what it is that you are saying right now, and as you say that right now, all the bits of you that need to hear it, every single conscious part of you, can become engrossed, and wrapped up, and engaged, in saying and hearing only that thing, so even though I might normally say that you can hear the sound of my voice on a conscious level, right now, all you can hear is the sound of your voice.

And as your unconscious mind is certain that your conscious self is only focused on and is only hearing the words that you are saying and the sound of your own voice and is completely disregarding anything that I'm saying go ahead and let your left hand and arm rise up and go ahead and touch your chin. And then fall back down into your lap taking you even more deeply into trance

[DJ's hand and arm do this. DJ is still repeating the mantra.]

And as you find yourself in that state where you keep saying that mantra, where that's *the* thing that you say, where that's *the* thing that you hear, where that's *the* words that you know right now, where my stuff is just sliding on by, I'm going to tell you another phrase, or something. I know…

Drinking water's really good, isn't it? You notice how easily you find yourself getting more and more thirsty, really wanting and needing to make sure that you're hydrated. Does that have anything to do with any of those other triggers that you've already been given? I don't know. You can let me know at some point in time. But only as a new thought, as that occurs to you. And never as if that's something you've ever heard before. On the count of five, find yourself stopping saying that mantra, and coming up wide, wide awake. One... two... three... four... and five *Snap!* Wide awake.

DJ: Yeah...

LA: Yeah, what?

DJ: It's funny, because "Drumbeat," was one of the files I listened to when I was trying to find a dual track file just now, so that's the mantra I chose.

LA: There we go.

DJ: [Drinks, sighs.]

LA: So, I'd say that one works pretty well. I'd say that's pretty good for today.

DJ: I went pretty deep, and I have no idea if you were saying anything.

LA: Yay! You know, it's funny, because I do a lot of talking, and there are some times when it would be useful for people to remember exactly what I said, so that they know just how affected they are. But a part of me really hates that idea of fame, so I don't necessarily want people to remember what I said.

DJ: You don't want fame?

LA: No. Just fortune. I would like a nice trust fund baby life, if I could have my druthers. Then I could do all sorts of off-the-grid home building, start new businesses, travel and exciting stuff like that. And no one would know who I was. No one would care. It'd be just fine. It'd all be good.

DJ: [Takes a drink. Sighs loudly.]

LA: [Laughs.]

DJ: I think, for me, there's something about the mantra and the countdown, that is very effective, in terms of putting me under. It could just be getting better and better training as a subject. But there was definitely something that felt a lot deeper about those trances.

LA: Do you think it's because you're participating in a different kind of way?

DJ: Yeah, I think so. Instead of giving my conscious mind something to think about, it's giving me something to do. In a physical sense. And I think there's that participation. I think there might be something to that.

LA: OK. I think that's a really useful thing, and I think that's why, when someone gets interrupted in the middle of doing something, and finds themselves doing something else—

[DJ drinks. Can be heard moaning slightly.]

—that can also be a really effective thing as well. However, so you'll notice now that when I take a drink of water, you're stopping, but you're remembering that you're stopping. So there's not like this whole moment where you're like, "Oh, I didn't stop." So I have to say that I don't think that that one is working particularly well for you. And maybe because we talked about it a whole lot. I'm not certain. What I'm wondering is now that I've noticed that, if your unconscious mind could actually go, 'Oh yeah, I was supposed to forget what we were doing in that moment." and then make you forget it.'

DJ: OK. We could, but we never talked about me forgetting when that happened.

LA: Well, we did, because we just changed what you were doing but not how it was supposed to work.

DJ: Oh! OK, because what I think what mind interpreted it as, was just doing the "Pause" trigger.

LA: Oh, I see.

DJ: As opposed to a "Freeze" trigger, I guess.

LA: No, no. It's not a freeze trigger at all. It was just, basically… it's interrupting someone in the middle of something. So when you see me do that, whatever you're in the middle of, you get interrupted, so you're not clapping your hands and saying anything, but your action should still be the same, which is, "I get interrupted because of this, I forget what's going on, and then when it's done, I go right back to where I was without the conscious understanding of what went on in that loop."

DJ: OK. Because I think that prior to that, my brain had interpreted it as a simple "Pause" trigger whenever you took a drink.

LA: And I'm fine with that, as a trigger. But as an amnesia trigger, it's not as effective.

DJ: No, definitely not.

LA: So let's see how well your mind can make that switch go on from now on. Because I'm pretty sure it could.

DJ: Yeah, I'm pretty sure it could, too.

LA: [Laughs. Takes a drink of water.]

So I think this is part of the fun of this. What we're experiencing sort of live and in person, with these things is a really cool look at how these things function, and how they work. Like, I tell people sometimes that humans are programmable, but hypnosis is really that—and when I say hypnosis, and I should clarify that, there're a lot of definitions, when I say it I mean, a trance-state where you are suggestible and you are open to my suggestions. And having someone be open to suggestion doesn't necessarily require trance, but it does require being open to the suggestion. And when I say "Open" I mean in a way where you say "Yes, I'm going to follow along with this," or, "No, I'm not going to follow along with this." Depending on how safe you feel the suggestion is for you, obviously. But I like where we get to the point where because humans are programmable, we can adjust these things as we go along and make them more effective.

## Notes

DJ: I chose the Drumbeat mantra largely because my iTunes got stuck playing it a short time earlier. One question would be whether it's more effective to have the mantra relate to the suggestibility (i.e., would a mantra of repeating the first line of "Jabberwocky" be just as effective of repeating "My mind will forget what it wants to forget"?). I found this extremely effective as a hypnotic technique, as well as a means of forgetting/not registering what was being said to me.

# CHAPTER TWENTY-ONE

## *Experiment 21 Dual Inductions, Multiple Track Audios*

***Ms Mesmer heard us.***
***One in each ear, talking low.***
***She forgot it all.***

***Two voices confound***
***Echo through my shattered mind***
***Fragments drift away***

As we've noted several times in several different scenarios, it is generally an effective technique in inducing hypnotic amnesia to overload the conscious mind so that it cannot easily register memory impressions.

A very effective way to do it, but one that is not available to everyone is via a dual induction. In a dual induction, the subject sits between two (or more) hypnotists. The hypnotists can, if they so choose, each do their own inductions and suggestions. Often, the two hypnotists will work together, coordinating their words and phrases. When it's done well, it is as close to free-form jazz as you're likely to find in the hypnotic world.

As a subject, it can be a very effective means of attaining a trance. Lee and DJ recommend the use of dual inductions for those who have a hard time going into trance or claim that they are 'too analytical.' By providing two distinct voices, the hypnotists ensure that the conscious mind is overwhelmed or quite simply bypassed. The conscious mind is generally incapable of following both voices and either chooses one to 'listen to' or else quite simply just shuts down.

Another way to achieve a similar effect is to listen to mp3 recordings which involve dual or even multiple tracks. Some of those are available on Lee's website.

Here, Lee and DJ perform a dual induction on a friend of theirs, Ms. Mesmer, who had never actually experienced this kind of induction before.

EXPERIMENT 21 DUAL INDUCTIONS SCRIPT

| Lee | DJ | Ms. M |
|---|---|---|
| And so we'll talk about it again, which is to say we're going to be doing a dual induction. Me on one side of your ear, DJ on the other. And our goal is to find that without too many additional suggestions about forgetting or amnesia, your unconscious mind simply lets go of what we said while you're in the trance state. Hopefully by the end you will not remember a piece of information that we'll give you and we'll figure out whatever that is when we get there. | | |
| | Right. | |
| Are you ready? | | |
| | | Yes. |
| Excellent. | | |
| | Excellent. | |
| And as you hear our voices… | | |
| | So you remember this feeling. | |
| Pouring into your ears… | | |
| | It's such a good feeling. | |
| Notice how simple it becomes to let your conscious self drift away. Notice how easy | The feeling of trance. | |
| | It's that feeling of letting go. | |

| | | |
|---|---|---|
| your unconscious mind comes closer and closer to our voices and picks up our words. And simply make the things we are saying what exactly happens to you. And as you find yourself in that state where your body gives in and your mind simply lets go. Notice how good it is to find yourself more deeply in this state right here. So comfortable against the sofa, paying attention to the sound of our voices and letting your conscious self only hear the sound of our voices and letting every single word that we say slide right on through to your unconscious mind. So easily and so effortlessly in a way that lets you know how effortlessly you find yourself deeply, deeply in trance. | You know how to get there. You know the best way to get there. Your unconscious mind knows the best way, to take you down. Clearly, simply, so that all you hear is the sound of our voices. The sound of our voices taking you down. Whether it's slow or whether it's fast; it doesn't matter. | [Relaxed Mmms.] |
| | Every word taking you down. Effortlessly taking you down whether it's fast or slow it doesn't matter, whatever is best. | [Satisfied Hmm.] |
| And as you find yourself here we're going to give you a piece of information for your mind to hold onto. And we're going to give you a piece of information to hold onto except I'm going to have you remember the same piece of information as | Whatever is best for you to give you the most pleasure, the nicest feeling taking you down, taking you deeper. | |

| | | |
|---|---|---|
| before. And that information is DJ's zip code–10101–which, again, is a palindrome. | | |
| | 10101. | |
| And then your unconscious self can simply hold onto that, and as it holds onto that it prevents your conscious self from ever knowing what that information is. And then because your unconscious self is holding onto it, knowing at some point in time it will get to have that information for your conscious self, you can feel yourself just doing those things. | That's it. | |
| | That would be so much fun to hold that back from yourself. To let your unconscious mind hold onto that 'til we tell you to remember and only until then will you hold onto it from your conscious self. | [Mmmms.] |
| And so as you find yourself in that state of hearing both of our voices again, going more effortlessly into trance. | | |
| I'm taking your unconscious mind's agreement right now for granted, although we did talk about this before. So as you find yourself right here, come back on "ten." Just forgetting what we've said while you were deeply in here on any sort of conscious level. | Right now. | |
| | Yes, even though we told you that number before, you still don't remember. | |

| | | |
|---|---|---|
| One. Two. Three. | | |
| | Four. Five. Six. Seven. | |
| Four. Five. Six. Seven. | | |
| Eight. Nine. Ten. Wide awake. | Eight. Nine. Ten. Wide awake. | |
| | | Wow. |
| [Laughter.] | [Laughter.] How's that stereo effect? | |
| | | I like it. |
| You like it? | | |
| | Yeah it's a lot of fun. | |
| I think… it looked about that way. | Well first off, how much of the trance do you remember? The second time around. Were you deeper than before? | [Sighs.]

I feel like I went down a lot faster, too. Wow. |
| It's like magic. | | |
| | Isn't it? So we started the trance, obviously, and could you hear the noise from outside? | |
| | | No was there…? |
| She won't pay attention to those voices when we're speaking in her ears. | | |
| | I just want to make sure! Well, they were clapping outside.

And so from trance 'til | |

| | you woke up do you remember anything? | |
| --- | --- | --- |
| | | Oh... no. |
| That's fascinating... | | |
| | And is that usual when you go into trance? | Yeah. |
| | And have you ever done a dual trance before? | Yeah. |
| | And has that ever happened when you've done dual trances? | No. |
| Because I'm super lazy so I just gave you the same information again! | Alright, and this time around we gave you some information. | |
| | OK, do you have a recollection of the information we gave you the first time around? | Ummm... spotty, yeah. |
| | That's OK! | |
| | Yup. So we know that you had a recollection of it between the two trances, right? | I don't know. I really don't. |
| | Alright and do you remember anything about that information? | No... I don't know. |

|  | Where did it go? | |
|  | | It's all gone!<br>Give it back! |
| You have to say please. | | |
|  | | Please? |
|  | No say it again. | |
| There's two of us… | | |
|  | Seriously you have to<br>say it at least twice. | |
|  | | Please? |
|  | OK, that's good. | |
|  | Well, the word that we<br>gave you to get the hint<br>was "palindrome."<br>Does that…<br>Ring any bells? | |
| Does that bring anything<br>back this time? | | |
|  | | No. |
| Nothing at all. | | |
|  | Nothing at all? Oh that<br>is interesting because<br>last time we gave you<br>that one, you went "that<br>means it's a number." | [Laughter.] |
| Yeah, your unconscious<br>mind said "That means a<br>number's involved,"<br>whereas your conscious<br>self …? | | |
|  | Do you remember even<br>telling us all that? | |
|  | | No. |
| So have that all back<br>now. | Remember.<br>For the record she's | |

| | making a face while all the memories are flooding back in. | |
|---|---|---|
| | | It's your zip code: 10101 |
| | Yes. | |
| Congratulations. | | |
| | That's right! | |
| | | That is so weird. |
| And yet it's fascinating. | | |
| | [Mmhmms] [To Ms. Mesmer] She (Lee) gets to see that all the time, when we play with amnesia where she'll take something away from me and I'm like 'ugh what is... I know it's something there' and she'll say 'remember now' and I'm like 'ah that's right, it's so simple!' | |
| | | Cool, it's like a light switch. |
| Yeah and in fact it's an interesting way to look at it because one of the thing we're doing is a forget switch. An on and off forget switch. And so that your brain does that automatically is really cool. Or did that automatically. | | |
| | | My brain tends to really take hold of suggestions and make them my own. |
| We like that. | | |

Yes we do.
That's incredible. Well thank you so much.

Yes we really appreciate it and your help too.

[Whispers] I didn't do anything...
Maybe look adorable.

Yes, you have, and we've got that on record now so if you ever need that again... and just to clarify, when we asked you to remember the second time around, you couldn't remember any of it. Now that we told you to remember do you remember it from the first time–the conversation from the first time–so it all, all that came back in? And until that point it wasn't even there?

Yeah, no, I remember waking up and the feeling of "I know this" but it wasn't really there. I was like "What do I know and what were we talking about?" And then the second time that you said it I was like "Oh there's another piece of my life that came back."

| | That's great! Well thank you so much. | |
|---|---|---|
| I think it's really fun for you to do this. Because usually I'm the one doing this, asking all these questions, and you're like "What, I don't remember...did we do that?" So the interrogation side is pretty interesting. | | |
| | It is.<br>I am a switch, so I like to do the interrogation sometimes, too. | |
| I know!<br>Thanks. | Thank you, thanks. | Thank you. |

## Notes

LA:   When I first started making audio recordings, I made very clean recordings–just my voice–and continued to do so for a long time. People often told me they were more effective for them than some of the audios with music or other distractions (as they referred to them), which prevented them from going into trance as deeply as they hoped. I know that it can sometimes be the closest thing to being hypnotized in person—the intimacy of one voice, whispered or spoken close to your ear.

I'm not the world's greatest subject—I can go intro trance easily, almost effortlessly, as I do that almost every time I hypnotize someone, but as for responding to suggestion, it is more challenging. A friend introduced me to Dr. Lloyd Glauberman's audios, and insisted that we listen to one together. The audio begins with a story of a train ride, and shortly into the audio adds another story in the other ear. Occasionally the stories collide. That is, one word is shared by both stories simultaneously. When I listened to that audio, I definitely lost track of time shortly after the second story joined in, and was lost in trance until the awakener. I experienced complete amnesia for the rest of the file. Having two different voices–one in each ear–was so effective for me that I then began to use multiple tracks in my own audios.

# CHAPTER TWENTY-TWO

## *Experiment 22 The Fade Away*

**Hold that thought clearly**
**Now see the edges less crisp**
**Dust falling sideways.**

So many of the experiments we've discussed in this book have been about distracting or overloading the conscious mind to allow the unconscious to take control. However, sometimes giving the unconscious a direct command can be effective as well. One of the tricks, of course, is not to just tell someone to forget something, but to give the mind, both conscious and unconscious, a task to hold on to.

Here, the unconscious mind is given the task of hiding the memories from the person as time goes on. This method enlists the unconscious mind to speed the forgetting thought process. Instead of memories fading over the course of days or months, the memories fade over the course of minutes.

In this case, the memories are allowed to remain for five minutes, and then, once the subject and the hypnotist move on to other topics, the memory "Fades away."

By allowing the conscious mind to initially experience the memory, and then by having the unconscious mind hide the memory, the entire mind is kept busy.

It's surprisingly effective, as we'll see:

LA:  Well, this is probably going to be very cruel, but…

Deep sleep! *Snap!* Right down, down, down, down, down, down, down, down, down, down.

I don't know what your unconscious mind is going to have your conscious self do right now. Perhaps your unconscious mind can put your conscious self in a state, whatever works best for your conscious self, where you simply holding on to nothing that I've said. Maybe we can coat your conscious self with Teflon! So things just sliiiiiiide right off it. Although it doesn't really matter for this particular trance. As you find yourself dropping so very deeply. *Snap!* So very deeply. *Snap!* So very deeply. *Snap!* So. *Snap!* Very. *Snap!* Deeply. *Snap!* Right now. You notice how very suggestible you are and what's going to happen during this particular trance is, when we're done, you're going to remember everything really clearly for about five minutes. And then, as I don't talk about it, and as we move on to other topics, anything that you actually do remember about this, simply, gently, fades away.

Until I specifically bring it up. Unless I specifically bring it up, it just disappears, leaving you only with the feelings of how good, deep, or exciting the trance was for you. And feel how good that is right now. Feel what that's like. And perhaps you can, I don't know, forget our little [embarrassing joke] incident. In the meantime, come all the way up on the count of five. One. Two. Three. Four. Five.

So I just thought of the number 27, which I sort of did here. Coating your conscious mind with Teflon.

DJ: OK. I had the experience of my conscious mind just trying to count numbers.

LA: Interesting. I gave you the instruction to have your unconscious have your conscious do something. That it thought was going to be effective for putting you in an amnesia state.

DJ: Oh. OK.

LA: Which is not really the same thing as what 22 is actually all about. But, that's OK.

DJ:  Should I know what 22 is?

LA: It really doesn't matter to me if you ever know. But you know.

DJ: Let's see if I have to look it up again.

LA: I'm going to have to put that as something different. I think we're up to 28 now. You know, when I started, I had twelve. So this has expanded. By quite a bit. Which is probably good. If we're writing a book, we want to make sure there's enough content in there, that people get something useful out of it. And I think that even though these have a similar end result, but not all exactly the same, and so I think there should be a little something for everybody, in and among these. If you're interested in hypnosis at all and you're not the kind of person that has somnambulism and forgets, or doesn't remember everything anyway. Hopefully there will be something in here that people will want to play around with. And I really hope that, since we came up with a whole bunch of new things since we started this, and some of the new ideas came from inductions I was in the middle of which had nothing to do with the initial idea, people will have sparks and go, "Oh, what about this?" When they're doing inductions or suggestions on their own. I'm really hoping that inspires people.

DJ: One thing I was thinking of that would be fun to play with–similar to when they did the "Weeping Angel" scene, at NEEHU–is the "Silence" from "Doctor Who." To do something along those lines. And it'd be kind of interesting if you could do that. Give them a pen and have them mark every...

LA: Well, you know, today is Doctor Who's day for that. Do you have any marks?

DJ: Nope.

LA: Are they invisible?

DJ: Are the marks invisible? ... Oh. ...That's cruel and wonderful. Oh, very well-played. That would be pretty nifty.

LA: I'll put that in as 29, because people need more Who. We should definitely include Doctor Who in more things.

DJ: Absolutely. I'm not going to say no.

LA: Right, right.

I'm going to specifically put in "Have the unconscious mind have the conscious self do something the unconscious knows would cause it to have amnesia." Because I feel that that really isn't the "Fade Away." [Random discussion about placement of experiments.]

## Notes

DJ: Lee said this didn't work as intended. Looking back, I would have thought it did; I seem to recall remembering more about the trance initially, and then it faded out as time when on.

# CHAPTER TWENTY-THREE

## *Experiment 23 Esdaile State*

### *Deeper than ever*
### *Disconnect from everything*
### *Healthy sleepy trance*

The Esdaile state is a type of intense and deep trance that has been known and written about since the 19th century.

James Esdaile was a Scottish Doctor who worked in India. He developed a technique for putting people into non-pharmaceutical anesthesia (indeed, this was from a time before chemical anesthesia) so that he could perform surgeries on them. His technique involved as much as ten to twelve hours of preparation work before the surgery. The technique was extremely successful, and, in fact, Esdaile found patients recovered quickly and had fewer complications. Esdaile used this to perform hundreds of surgeries.

Once entered, the state renders the subject completely non-responsive to outside stimuli. It is as if the brain almost entirely shuts off. It isn't quite a dream state— the subject will have no memories of what is occurring, because the higher functions of the brain are, for all intents and purposes, shut off. Restoring the subject's functioning requires something more than just yelling at the subject to wake up, or moving the subject—the subject is likely to remain non-responsive. Instead, prior to entering the state, the subject needs some kind of 'exit' trigger before beginning the process of dropping the subject. When Esdaile used this method, they would allow the subject to wake up naturally after their surgeries, allowing the body to heal itself well.

Today, we often don't have ten to twelve hours to prepare the subject for the state. However, if you are, or are working with, a responsive subject, this is a state–or one very close to it–that you can achieve with practice and repetition.

Lee was very successful with inducing the state in DJ, and has been able to return him to that state with a trigger.

Note that in the original state, Dr. Esdaile and his assistants would run hands or branches over the patients, using a kind of 'energy work' to place the patient into trance. During the induction, Lee did something similar to DJ while bringing him into trance.

As stated before, Lee and DJ both found this surprisingly effective.

LA: OK, so initially, James Esdaile or his physician assistants would take people and they'd lie the patients down. Then the PA would place their hands or branches above their bodies and run them up and down, using Magnetism (a popular idea of the day) to put people in trance.

DJ: Mhmm.

LA: Sometimes they would take leaves or branches or something and just draw it over the patient's body too, but the whole idea, they didn't really know what they were doing. But these patients ended up, these patients with severe medical issues that needed surgery, ended up in these trance states, that were SO profound, that sometimes they didn't come out of the trance until several days after the surgery.

Sometimes the patients would just be almost catatonic, but the patients would be operated on, they would have all sorts of stuff done to them… and they'd get to this state, the PA would do their thing to the patients with their hands or branches or whatever, and leave the patients there, until someone would come back and check to see if they were ready for surgery. It might be hours, and in that time, the patients were sort of sinking themselves more deeply and completely into that state. The Esdaile state was named after him by David Elman, but he (Esdaile) didn't call it that.

DJ: OK.

LA: We have a couple of advantages here (to get you, DJ into that state). One is that we're not actually going to be doing surgery (laugh), and we still want you to be able to experience the depth of trance…

DJ: Right.

LA: …that those patients got to experience. And of course we have advantages because we're a little bit more technologically and artistically advanced in going into trance—you have really good skills in that area already. But basically patients could literally be cut into, loud noises could happen, patients could be adjusted, (Elman removed a lot of large tumors and did a few amputations) and all sorts of things could go on and patients would be oblivious to it, to all of it. I mean, literally oblivious on every single possible level and, which is why some of those patients (whom Esdaile operated on) took a couple of days to wake up.

DJ: Which raises the obvious question, "How do you wake someone up from that state?"

LA: Well, a couple of different things; some patients would actually just need the doctor to forcefully say "Wake up now!" and some part of their brain would do that. On the other hand, Esdaile noticed that patients who were in these states healed better, so sometimes staying in that state until you're healed/healing is a good thing because your brain is just automatically taking care of you in that way.

I'm not certain if his assistants or he **ever** talked to people about getting them in that sort of state. Esdaile did feel that the patients were inferior sometimes they were in different social castes, sometimes there was a language barrier and the patients wouldn't have understood him. And so it (consent) just became unimportant.

I think I talked a little bit with you before about how he talks about how this is non-consensual, he's doing things to the patients that were non-consensual. And yet—he had a woman he operated on, he removed her tumor, and she didn't know what was going on. They put her in trance, removed the tumor, waited for her to come out of the trance. She healed pretty quickly, went home, but the tumor grew back because sometimes they do that. She had to return for additional surgery, but this time, they'd told her what had been done to her before the last surgery, the trance state they put her in for the operation, etc., and when she came back for the second surgery, she would not go into trance, and did not go through the surgery as well, it was traumatic, she was screaming, it was painful Anesthesia was not available at that time. It was way before they were using ether on a wide scale basis and she didn't feel as well or heal as well: it was more traumatic.

So it became more important to operate with the patients **in** that state without consent as opposed to either doing the surgery without the patients being in trance (as it caused considerable more pain, trauma and slower healing) or overcoming the barriers to doing the surgery quickly by finding someone who could speak the patient's language.

So this state, because you already have the ability to go into trance, your unconscious mind will not register pain, you'll find yourself dropping down more and more deeply, and look at you, you're already adept at going deeply into trance, but you know, you're likely to be completely oblivious. I don't want to project amnesia onto you because that's one of the things we're testing for.

DJ:  OK.

LA:  But that was generally the experience of the people who were in that state. Even though we only have a short amount of time, we should be able to get you into that state, and then literally be able to do almost anything to you. And for you to not notice it at all. I will probably use "Wake up now!" so your unconscious can literally shut out everything else. Once you get there, other than going more firmly into that state, which you can do on your own, and that phrase "Wake up now!" which you can use to come out. And I'm pretty sure your unconscious can pay attention to that and just go, OK, that's fine, whatever I do, because I will be pinching you or hitting you a little bit…

DJ:  Sure, sure.

LA:  …to see what kind of responses there are, but your conscious will probably not even notice it, and if you do bruise a little bit, your unconscious can just heal you faster, because that's a part of this state.

So—ready?

DJ:  Yes.

LA:  Deep sleep. Except even deeper sleep.

Now, I've already talked about what it's like to be in that state, what that place is like. And I know your unconscious is really good, really, really good, at making my words your reality, but as you find yourself in that state, as you find your self approaching that state, as you understand what it's going to take, for you to be there, for you to be so completely out of it that you're just non-responsive, that things just let go.

It's as though all of your senses have been disconnected, right now your sense of hearing is fine, but at some point in time, even that's going to go, and at some point in time, you're going to notice how simply you sink down into that state where pinches on the back of your hand are just non-existent;

Where you don't feel if I whack you;

Where you're literally, and I mean that in the very best sense of the word, not here in any way that matters regarding your senses.

You're still alive, breathing, heart beating, unconscious mind functioning, but you're going to drop now deeper, letting go, and perhaps even some part of you is going to find that you end up in this state really simply.

[Picks up his arm and lets it drop firmly, several times in a row.]

As you go down more now.

I don't know which state you can find yourself letting go of most easily, but there's your ability to sense and to feel, whether it's your ability to see, even light might be something you're oblivious to, your sense of taste, of smell. Dinner's cooking, but it becomes irrelevant but as you notice that you stop feeling, my hand, the sofa, the temperature, and you find yourself in that state of dropping down so deeply where your body just decides it can (drops arm again) give in. Where nothing else matters except YOU DROPPING into that state where THESE parameters are being met.

We're fortunate that we both speak English, at least reasonably so. But just to be a little more historically accurate (at this point, Lee reaches over and begins to run her hands down over DJ's body, a few inches above, in a sweeping motion from head to toe.) I'll wave my hands over your body so that your... electrical field perhaps, can notice the field, and can sweep you down more completely, so that you're just completely gone. Not *here*.

[Lee claps loudly right at DJ's ear.]

Irrelevant to pain...

[Second clap.]

Loud noises...

[Third clap.]

Nothing fazes you; you're just not *here*.

[Lee runs a butter knife over DJ's forearm.]

This could be a sharp, sharp scalpel... and yet, nothing.

One of the fascinating things about this is that a surgery, Esdaile's patients often bled less.

This is an excellent state for going to the dentist, for example, for you to be able to self induce, if you were told ahead of time, to be able to open your mouth up wide, and just hold it there during the dentist's operations. Notice how fascinating it would be for the dentist even if you could control your drooling, your blood. Your unconscious can do all these things, amazingly.

And you can just notice, how simple it is again, for you to just let go of that pain to let go of any sensation, [*Snap!*] sound, all the these things just go. We can get there much more quickly now. We don't need twelve or five hours, we don't need one hour for someone to lie and wait, and of course, dinner is coming soon.

So hold on unconsciously, to how easy it is to get here, and let's come up with something that will allow you to get HERE, where you are right now, really easily.

I'm going to plant that seed, because your unconscious is still paying a little bit of attention. Even though you're not responding on any sort of level right now.

Just lying in wait for what comes. And I think what we'll say is "Invoke Esdaile State."

And then of course, DJ, "Wake up now!"

[Six minutes to Esdaile state and back again.]

DJ:     WOW! I started doing a countdown in my mind to go deeper and I lost track after that.

[Lee chuckles.]

LA:    So it's really fascinating it isn't… That was not very long at all, I mean, it was like ten minutes we were talking for some of that before, and maybe five to seven minutes ?

DJ:    OK.

LA:    So that's a really profound state of trance to be in (so quickly).

DJ:     Yes.

LA: I totally picked your whole hand and arm up by pinching the skin on the back of your hand, so I apologize.

DJ: Nonononono.

LA: And I slapped you here. [Indicating DJ's arm.]

DJ: It's OK; it's fine.

LA: And with even more time you could literally walk in and find someone catatonic, totally immobile, no matter the position they were placed in. I talked about going to the dentist, and can give you this as a self trigger, but I think it we could have tested it while you were in it, not after we woke you up.

DJ: It was very startling. It was a bit of a shock waking up, it was not the usual count up.

LA: It was sudden, for one, and it was louder, for two. The goal behind that, if I had set a secret phrase, other than that, for example, that no body else knew, only slightly problematic if I keeled over dead it would be interesting to see how long it would take for someone to come out of that, and that might be an interesting experiment to do at some other point in time. But the point is to figuratively strip away your senses, so that what's left is...

DJ: Nothing, essentially.

LA: Yeah, it's a wearable body that can have stuff done to it. Now if someone wasn't as good a subject it would take longer or more effort.

DJ: Sure.

LA: I like to describe what I'm going to do, and then when I put you in trance, your unconscious mind can just go, "Oh, I'll make that happen." Not everyone is that blessed, some people like to be in that unconscious state where they take words in, as opposed to any place taking words in.

DJ: ...Right.

LA: [Laughs.]

DJ: I'm still kinda waking up, that's a very strange feeling. It felt really deep, I don't remember anything that really happened, I think my unconscious has a VAGUE recollection. I can sort feel it in the background, like things happened, and there was some movement but that's it.

LA:  Well again, for a really short-duration demonstration, that's a really profound kind of depth of trance that you can get to.

DJ:  As a hypnotist, was there something you were doing differently to bring out that state?

LA:  Well, we talked about it ahead of time, and I had you shut down your senses.

DJ:  OK.

LA:  So that's not something we normally do and it was also a direct command not like when we do this (flashed a shiny ring) and your brain just kind of goes, "Hey... there's something" so that's a different kind of thing. And I clearly stated it, but I don't think you have to, because Esdaile couldn't communicate with a lot of his patients.

I was doing some of this...

DJ:  [Into the microphone] And by "this," she's running her hands over my electrical field.

LA:  So I thought I'd throw some of it in because it worked for hundreds of their patients and I thought, "It can't hurt."

DJ:  That's great.

[Pause.] Yeah, pretty much from somewhere in the induction to when you woke me up there's a scene missing.

LA:  So it does cause amnesia.

DJ:  Yes. I would have guessed it was about 30 seconds between when I lost count and when you woke me up.

LA:  Wow. That's the biggest time gap we've had, I think, that you've experienced for that.

DJ:  Yeah.

LA:  So to bring you back there, we have some time, let's bring you back there.

DJ:  OK.

LA:  Invoke Esdaile State and just see how you can get there.

DJ:  [Drops.]

[Lee may have done more of the hands over the electrical field. Lee also does some catalepsy testing with arm. DJ lets him drift for about a minute or two.]

LA: DJ, wake up, now!

[DJ wakes up.]

LA: How did that feel?

DJ: [Woozily.] That's really deep.

LA: In two minutes, really deep.

DJ: Wow, that's some powerful stuff—I had a vague notion that you pinched my hand.

LA: And that's the thing—theoretically you shouldn't experience any of those things at all, and I was thinking, would his arms just stay, so I lifted them up, and I had to say stay, and they did, and that was really cool, so that means some part of you is still paying attention. And really, your unconscious mind is very attentive so I would expect something like that.

DJ: If you're going for that, might it be worth it to say to the conscious self, "We're going to ask you to shut yourself down for a little while until these words come through."

LA: That still means they have to filter. If I were Erickson... for example, he has this video where he's talking with a woman and her arm is out like this (holds arm out) and he asks her how it feels. "It tingles." she says. "It's single." he replies "No, it tingles." she says then all of a sudden her arm feels separate from her body. So I feel if I were to use those kind of words instead, your brain might have done something along those lines, and gone "It's separate, what does that mean, I can't move it? Because it's not part of me anymore." That's something to explore.

DJ: After a certain point, when you put me under the second time, under than a vague... I think the pinch came through.

LA: Yeah, but that was like 30 seconds in. To get even to that place, where you might have remembered something, in that short a time. What if you had been gone for 45 minutes or an hour? Would something that had happened that long ago still be in any part of your awareness?

DJ: I can imagine probably not, given how powerful that felt.

LA: Now you have something brand new and shiny to think about!

DJ: I know, thank you!

LA: Thank *you*!

## Notes

DJ: This—more than any other method we've explored before or since—had a profound impact on my memory. By which I mean, I have no recollection of anything happening between beginning when Lee started telling me about the state and when she woke me up. The first few times we did it, in fact, coming out of the trance felt like being plunged through a window, so shocking did it feel.

Lee worked with me on that, so that coming out of the Esdaile state would be less traumatic.

I can say that she tells me she used the Esdaile state on me when she was taking me to the airport. And I did lose what was probably a 20-minute drive.

She also, shortly after this recording, used a medical needle on my arm (we had pre-negotiated this) while I was in the state. I can tell you that I have no recollection that the needle was placed in my skin, and that it is extremely disconcerting to have what can only be described as a shift in perception—like that moment between blinks—and then seeing a goddamn needle in your arm. Interestingly, I am told that most people experiencing needles have an endorphin rush as a result of the needle. I can tell you that I did not experience that rush.

In any event, Lee will have to tell you more, because I don't think I could even reliably tell you how many times, when or for how long I've been in this state.

Suffice it to say that I found it very, very powerful.

LA: DJ has been in this state several times, with or without anesthesia testing. I don't have an exact tally of how many times I've used it, but each time, no matter how long the trance was, he exhibits all the same signs.

# CHAPTER TWENTY-FOUR

## *Experiment 24 Forget Switch*

***Root implementing***
***Toggle data storage off***
***Machine fantasies***

One of Lee's favorite things to do with her more responsive subjects is to have the subject discover the "Control Room" in their mind. It's a fantastic shortcut for allowing all kinds of subtle or drastic changes in a person's psyche.

Once the subject is in an altered state, Lee guides them into their unconscious mind and leads them into a room. Lee tells the subject that it is a "Control Room," with dials, knobs, switches, gauges, but otherwise, the subject is free to imagine what their own "Control Room" looks like.

Lee leads the subject into the room and has them go to a specific place inside. Then she has the subject adjust dials and throw some switches. For example, for a subject who wants to experiment with being less inhibited, she may lead them to a panel on which there is an "Inhibitions" dial. She asks the subject what the setting is. Let's say the subject says the dial is set at 'eight out of ten.' Lee may asks the subject to adjust the dial to 'seven' or 'six,' or whatever the subject is comfortable with. Lee will have a button light up that says "ACTIVATE? Yes or No" and asks the subject to choose one or the other. As the subject leaves the "Control Room," Lee will ask the subject, once again, to answer "ARE YOU SURE? Yes or No?" on the way out the door. In this way, the subject has accepted whatever the suggestion is twice over.

Lee has used this to raise or lower many, many things, including suggestibility, pride, confidence, orgasmic ability, 'snarkiness' and submissiveness.

Any time she leads the subject to the "Control Room," she always notes that there are certain switches and levers that should never be touched, and that if anyone tries to touch those levers or switches, the subject can just ignore those attempts or otherwise wake up.

In the following transcript, Lee places two 'switches' in the DJ's "Control Room," one for "Forget" and one for "Scopolamine." At one point, Lee actually turns both of them on. Let's see how that worked out.

LA:  DJ, deep sleep. All the way down. Just noticing how good it feels. And, actually, I don't know if you're going to go all the way down or not. I mean, I imagine you'll find yourself feeling very deeply in a trance, whatever that means to you. And, that your conscious self is probably going to stop paying a lot of attention to what it is that I'm doing. It focuses a lot more on how good it feels to be where you are. How nice it is to just be in that state of hypnotic trance. And how it's really fun to just be there, no matter what else is going on around you. But as you find yourself in this state, as your unconscious mind comes a little closer and holds you in that right place to be to be as suggestible as necessary to make the things that I say work with you and for you, let your unconscious mind take you to a corridor deep within your mind. And there're a lot of doors and doorways. And somewhere in this corridor there's a plain door with a plain plaque on it, and it just says "Control Room." When you find that "Control Room," just reach up and touch your chin. And then let your hand drop.

[DJ does this.]

LA:  Thank you.

Go ahead and open this door and go into this room. The door will shut behind you. And while you're here, take a look around. This place is full of conduits and computers and bookcases and files. Maybe it looks like a library, maybe it looks like something totally different. I have no idea. Your room looks like whatever you want it to look like. But I do know this. On the wall there are panels, with knobs, switches, dials, sliders… and these hold the key to *you*.

Now there are things in this room that neither you, nor I, nor anyone else should ever touch. And that's really important so I'm going to say it again.

There are things in this room that neither you, nor I, nor anyone else should ever touch. And if anyone ever does try to touch them, or tries to get you to touch them, and if any of these are bad for you or are slippery slopes that could lead to tragedy, you'll notice that you'll wake up and that person will be unable to hypnotize you again, or, as your brain's pretty qualified at knowing what's good for you and what's not, you can simply allow it to reject those suggestions, or to adjust them to something you're OK with. Whether your unconscious mind makes it an obvious objection by raising your hand or whether it does or says something else, notice your mind knows the difference between the things we do, whether it be for good or for fun or both and the things that might not necessarily be so healthy for you.

I'd like you to find your way over to one of the panels on the wall. Then I'd like you to find your way over to the panel marked, "Memory." When you find that panel marked "Memory," notice there is a little toggle switch there that says "Forget, On or Off." Right now it's probably in the middle. So right now you do whatever it is that you normally do. I'd like your mind to pay attention to this, and to know this: that from now on, whenever I–and only I–say to you, whether you're fully conscious or deeply in trance, "Forget Switch On," that switch right there will automatically go to the 'On' position for whichever particular point in time it is that I'm working with your unconscious to get you to forget something. Whether you're hypnotized or whether you're wide awake. Now it will only forget from the moment the switch goes 'On' until I say "Forget Switch Off."

And it's only to induce amnesia for a certain specific thing. As long as your unconscious mind is OK with that happening–and I have no nefarious plans, above and beyond my usual fun, nefarious plans–go ahead and let me know that you're OK with activating that switch, whenever I say "Forget Switch On" or "Forget Switch Off," by just reaching up and touching your chin, and letting your hand fall back down for me.

[DJ does this.]

LA:  Thank you.

So hold onto that. Notice that when you're done, a button pops up that says "Activate: Yes or No?" It's a big, green button. You can choose to activate it, 'Yes' or 'No.' Go ahead and hit it if you are interested in activating this particular trigger.

And then, go ahead and head over to the door. Another button pops up and says "Are you sure? Yes or No." No matter which one you pick, the door's going to open for you. So go ahead and say aloud, "Yes" or "No." And notice how the door opens for you.

DJ:  Yes.

LA: Thank you. You can step through the door and it will shut behind you. And, as you find yourself, in that hallway in that corridor, go ahead and find a room, one that's filled with furniture [sic], and take a seat.

And as you find yourself getting comfy, let's do a quick check of what exactly this trigger does.

So, DJ, Forget Switch On. *Snap!*

And while you're here, and that "Forget Switch" is on, I can tell you all sorts of things. I want to make sure that I only tell you things that will only be good to be forgotten. And are really only helpful for the purposes of our testing. So, let's see. I'm going to tell you something that you probably don't know, and it doesn't really matter. But I will tell you right now that I am a "Spider Solitaire" junkie. And you can just forget that I've told you that because your "Forget Switch" is on.

Forget Switch off. *Snap!*

And then, come on out of that chair, and walk back down that corridor and on the count of ten, notice that you're just walking yourself up out into complete and absolute consciousness. One, two, three, four, feeling better, feeling so good, five, six, seven, eight, nine and ten. Wide awake.

[Pause.] Hi.

DJ: Hi.

LA: OK. So. How was that?

DJ: That was good.

LA: What do you remember about that?

DJ: I remember the "Control Room," the "Forget Switch." I think you checked twice to see if it was OK?

LA: Yes.

DJ: You had me go into an empty room full of furniture [sic].

LA: Yes.

DJ: And then... I guess something happened, and then I was waking up.

LA: OK. So when you said "I guess something happened," what do you mean by that?

DJ: I don't know why you put me into an extra room without something else happening.

LA: Oh. Because it's the aftercare room. Everyone goes there.

[Laughter.]

After you go to the "Control Room," you always go to that room. Well, not that room, but one of the rooms down there.

OK. So. I'm thinking that this particular trigger could have an additional part to it. And it could be a trigger that will allow you to remember what happened while the switch was on. But I'm not quite sure yet the best way to go about it. Let's see, Forget Switch on. I like cashmere socks. Forget Switch Off.

[DJ looks slightly perplexed. Lee laughs.]

DJ: What?

LA: [Laughs some more.]

DJ: Are you having fun?

LA: Well, no, I was just had a bad thought just pop into my head, and I had to slap myself down.

DJ: But why?

LA: No, no. I've agreed that I won't, for the most part, torment you with those things. So I can't say them.

DJ: Who said that?

LA: I've agreed to myself, that I will be as kind as I can. [Laughs.] Oh, what's the fun in that, I know.

DJ: "For purposes of science…"

LA: Oh, right. Let's see. For purposes of science, then, Forget Switch on. And it might be really great if you could forget that I actually said that, or that, and for that. And, let's see, [your soccer team] really sucks. And then Forget Switch Off.

DJ: My subconscious is really unhappy with you right now.

LA: I'm so sorry, please forgive me.

DJ:   I have a suspicion for why that might be the case.

LA:   Please, forgive me, unconscious.

DJ:   For purposes of science...

LA:   Yes, for purposes of testing...

DJ:   I'm going to let it go.

LA:   I'm trying to figure out if there are other things that you feel strongly about, that we can...

DJ:   Well, like [my soccer team] I feel pretty strongly about.

LA:   Right, but there are other things, other than that, that we can use so we don't get that whole kind of response.

DJ:   [Seriously.] Did you say something about [my soccer team]?

LA:   Yes.

DJ:   Oh.

LA:   Because that's kind of a give-away, and I'd like to not say things that might be a giveaway. On the other hand, I can imagine it would be sort of weird for someone to not recognize that something has been said, but still have that feeling of what's been said. And so, I'm certain that your unconscious mind can take those feelings and sort of dampen them down, too. And maybe in the interest of maybe having that whole experience, that would be a useful thing. But I don't know if I want to go in that direction.

I mean, if we really are doing absolute amnesia, you wouldn't actually have a feeling; there'd be nothing there, it'd be a flat-line, as opposed to that "Oh!" response.

DJ:   Unless I'm mistaken, when you have the "Forget Switch" on I'm technically still conscious.

LA:   Yes!

DJ:   So we can interact.

LA:   Yes.

DJ:   And by interacting there will be possible emotions about that interaction. So if you bad-mouth a team I like, or if you say nasty things to me, or really cool things to me or whatever, then you stop, and I go from zero to seven on the emotional scale, whatever that emotional scale is, that can be kind of cool, because all of a sudden...?

I mean, you could go "Radio" to ten, and all of a sudden, I'll have no memory of that whatsoever, and then "Forget Switch Off," and then 'boom,' and I'm all turned on and then it's "What the hell?" where'd that come from?

But I can also see the virtue of... I mean, obviously, I'm a susceptible subject anyway, but there's no suggestibility with it. I mean, you can say things to me, and I'll forget it, but there're no suggestions that my unconscious will remember.

LA: Well, it should not allow your conscious self to remember. I mean, your unconscious mind knows a bunch of stuff that just never comes up. If you really needed to know something about something, it might just happen that way, but it doesn't really have to... So, I have a friend who says that his unconscious is like a six-year old with a secret. And that's fine in some instances. But it's not always fine. And your unconscious does do things for you and does protect you in many, many ways.

But sometimes it's just chugging along, not really paying much attention, so it doesn't have to pay a lot of attention, except I've asked it to pay a lot of attention to me when I speak, and so, you know, that sort of may be at cross-purposes for it. Because I don't want it to ignore what I'm saying. And I would also like it to have an unemotional response as much as possible, when there's that state going on. When the "Forget Switch" is on, then it's important that it behave as though, again, the flat-line of everything, and the experience is in this bubble down here that is under the surface that you don't even know is happening, because you're just moving on. So there's a thing that is left behind, and you just go on from that.

DJ: And this is one of those triggers that you can do a lot. You could make it a "Scopolamine Switch," in addition to not remembering what's going to happen, the person is very suggestible for that period of time as well. And then, "Scopolamine Switch Off" and you carry on your merry way.

LA: [Laughs.] "Mwahaha."

DJ: Exactly. And so,

LA: [Drinks water.]

DJ: [Pauses.] And so... Goodness, hypnosis is so much fun.

For a switch, much like other forms of hypnotic amnesia, you can match with other things or just use it on its own, and set everything up, it's probably helpful, for this thing in particular, are you trying to purge everything that happened for that period of time from the conscious memory, or carry something through.

LA: And I think that's a good point, because I think sometimes you might want to do one, and sometimes you might want to do the other. I don't have a particular preference.

[Later.]

The benefit that I like about having a trigger is that you don't have to describe all the things you want to get done, you can just set it once and let it go. And so, for example, if right now, I told your unconscious mind–as an example of a suggestion working–to go in and to know that there's also a "Scopolamine Switch" right next to the "Forget Switch" that will work exactly the same way that I told you, then I bet your brain is just making that happen right now. I don't know if you feel a change. I mean, my friend gets this electrical pulse thing going down his spine. I don't know if you have that, or something else going on, that let's you know, "Oh, a change has happened. My brain just made something happen." Some people might say "Yeah, that didn't really work for me." Some people might say that— and yet it did. And for others, they may say that, and it didn't. So, it's a, 'know your subject' kind of thing. And, obviously be willing to test and test and test until you know. Or until you've made it happen.

Those kinds of things.

DJ: It felt like a light trance, and then, for a few seconds, a bit of that light yummy endorphin feeling from when I go into a light trance. Like my subconscious was going "Oh…that's something I should be doing. OK. I'm on it."

LA: And that's a really powerful thing. I mean, to be able to say, "From now on, I'd like you to do this, so I'm going to install this right off the cuff." It's really thrilling to do that.

And since you suggested it, let's say Forget Switch on, DJ. *Snap!* Let's do "Radio" at one, two, three, four, five, six, seven, eight, nine. Forget Switch off.

DJ: [Audibly sighs.]

LA: …this is your idea; you deserve to have it done.

DJ: [Laughs.] Touché. Also, ironically, a déjà vu moment.

LA: How is that a déjà vu moment?

DJ: I don't know, sometimes I get déjà vu. Where I swear I had the memory of what just happened ages ago.

LA: Hmm. Interesting. Really?

DJ: Yep.

LA: That's pretty fascinating.

DJ: OK.

LA: I don't have anything against déjà vu.

DJ: I can only report that it happened and move on. [Drums his fingers.]

LA: What else?

I also like the idea of "Scopolamine Switch On." There's something about that that's really interesting. You probably respond in a slightly different way to that, because you feel like there's some sort of drug thing going on. So we can have a complete and absolute conversation about things right now, and it would just be completely gone by the time I turn that off, which is fascinating. Because you feel, right now, almost, like you're fully able to participate in whatever conversation that we might have.

DJ: Yes. I feel slightly, dopey, but definitely conscious and able to do stuff. Exactly like a little bit of a drug was put in my drink. So I'm thinking, "OK...sure! I want to agree with whatever you're going to tell me."

LA: [Laughs.]

DJ: ...more than I would usually want to agree with whatever it is you want to tell me.

LA: [Laughs.] Right... just more.

DJ: And it reminds me—

LA: [Takes a drink of water.]

DJ: Oy. Between that and being on "nine..."

[Both laugh.]

DJ: I may be giggling. It should probably be clear–or not–that on Scopolamine, I am receptive to just *your* suggestions as opposed to anyone else's. Have we already talked about that?

LA: I believe so. And if I haven't, let's make sure that it's there from now on.

DJ: [Pause.] Yes.

LA: You know, this is a lot of stuff that you've done. So we have a whole new toy box going on in your mind. And obviously, if you want to enjoy these things with other people, you can do that. For right now, it's locked down. Right now, it's my toy box. Let's just call it that. Right now, my toy box is in your head. And then after, when we've finished, then, go play, see what happens.

DJ: Oh god.

[Laughter.]

LA: Yeah... that could be dangerous.

DJ: It sounds like so much fun, and I am also scared at the same time.

LA: Yeah... I know. But don't worry. Let's say, Radio Off.

[DJ exhales.]

LA: And Scopolamine Off.

DJ: [Looks lost.]

LA: It's so effective. Oh, I really like that. I can tell by the expression in your face, you're like, "What the hell just happened?"

DJ: Yes.

LA: We had a conversation.

DJ: Did we?

LA: Yes. With a "Scopolamine Switch."

DJ: OK. Good.

LA: So, I can't tell you what happened. So you'll go listen to it and you'll be like, "Wow, what the hell was that?"

[Laughter.]

# CHAPTER TWENTY-FIVE

## *Experiment 25 Fractionation*

*Roller coaster toasts*
*Whatever's left of your brains*
*Memories at sea.*

For people experienced in the uses of recreational hypnosis, fractionation is going to be nothing new. But if you are a relative novice, some background information is definitely in order.

Often, when one comes out of a trance, there is a period of adjustment as someone reverts back to normal 'Awake' space. The subject isn't *quite* in a trance, but neither are they fully 'Awake.' In this period of time a person can still be a little suggestible. This is why 'Aftercare' after a hypnosis session is so important—it's not just about processing what happened, it can be about making sure nothing *new* happens that the subject isn't entirely prepared for.

Nevertheless, a hypnotist can take advantage of this brief period of waking suggestibility to send the subject right back into a trance. Subjects usually find this second trance to be much more encompassing and consuming than the previous trance. And, more to the point, every subsequent time a hypnotist brings the subject out of and back into trance, the subject often feels the trance as more and more profound each successive time. This process is called "Fractionation."

Generally speaking, a subject does not even have to come all the way out of trance in order to experience fractionation. The hypnotist can suggest that the subject comes half way out of trance before dropping all the way back deeper than they were before.

The profound effect of this is that the subject can feel a full-body trance. Moreover, the mind is very sluggish and can be slow for minutes–or even hours–

after the subject wakes up. As a result, fractionation can be a tool for forgetting what happens during the trance and in between fractionations, as we'll see here.

It should be noted also that it may be lost on the inexperienced subject (or hypnotist, for that matter) how profound an effect fractionation can have on one. Generally, subjects can often attest that after only two or three 'roller coaster rides,' the subject can experience extremely deep trance states. Let's see how many DJ experiences.

[Having just done a fractionation session, Lee and DJ realize that the recorder didn't capture the sessions.]

DJ:     I sort of have a dim… it feels like the dim recollection after you've woken up from a nap, and you know you've dreamt something. And you have a sketchy outline, but not the thing itself.

LA:     OK. So let's do fractionation again, then. No of course, this is fractionation of fractionation, so we'll see how far down you get.

        [DJ exhales, as if preparing for a hard struggle.]

        There you go.

DJ:     Ready for the roller coaster.

LA:     Yeah, I think that's what it's going to feel like.

DJ:     'Keep all brain cells inside the car at all times.'

LA:     Yeah. You don't want to lose those.

        DJ, deep sleep. *Snap!*

        That's right. And as you find yourself sinking down, again, let yourself head to that depth. Now, you've gone into an even deeper state of trance. But I know that your unconscious mind, once it knows how to get there, can go there [*Snap!* *Snap!* *Snap!* *Snap!*] much faster than it ever has before. So let it just take you there. Notice how quickly and effortlessly you find yourself there.

        That's right, just get as comfortable as you need to, adjust what you need to, and notice that you can just take yourself down so deeply into trance, that there's something about where you are right now, and where you're about to be, and where you're about to be after that, that begins to be faster and quicker and easier as you drop into trance more and more easily. As you find yourself dropping into trance more and more deeply, right now, let your unconscious mind, on the count of five, bring you up about 85% of the way. And then, drop you twice as deeply as you are right now as quickly as it possibly can, when I snap my fingers.

One, two, three, four, five. Awake.

Now you may or may not notice that you want to open your eyes. I know that I can put you in a state of waking trance, but we don't need to do that right now. Because your unconscious mind certainly can get you to the point. *Snap!*

Of just plunging you down more firmly right now. Twice as deeply down as you had been before. And then, on the count of five, come up about half way.

One, two, three, four, five. Awake.

That's right. And maybe it's just too much effort to even open your eyes at this point in time.

And then, deep sleep. *Snap!* Twice as deeply down as you were before.

And then feel what it's like to come up now. *Snap!* Wide awake!

That's right.

And then deep sleep. *Snap!*

All the way. Twice as deeply down as you were. And, again, the numbers are irrelevant almost. Your unconscious mind always knows how long it's going to take you. The distance between where you are and what wide awake is, and so it can figure out twice that, and drop you down more completely. And we don't have to drop you down a hundred times deeper or a thousand times deeper. Because your unconscious is infinite and has the ability to simply take you as deeply in, as far in, as it has the capacity for. And then...?

I just thought of something interesting.

However...wide awake on the count of five.

One, two, three, four, five. Wide awake.

[Slight pause.]

And deep sleep! *Snap!* Right now.

And let your unconscious mind right now, instead of taking you to the deepest level of trance that you've ever been in, let your unconscious mind, even though the space in there is infinite, let your unconscious mind take you to the end of your space.

I don't know what that means for you. I don't know if there are some boundaries in your mind in certain places. But I expect them to be far out or down. And so this is deeper than going into the deepest level of trance you've ever been. This is going to the furthest reaches of your unconscious mind. This is where there's an edge or a border. This time as you raise your arm, as you go there, letting me know that you've gone there all the way. And I know it might take a little bit longer than it took before. I also know that because it's farther it might also feel like it's the same amount of time. Because your unconscious mind becomes better and faster at getting you to these new places. So as you find your arm raising, as your unconscious mind gets you closer and closer to that space, that border, that edge of your mind. Inward, downward, upward, even. Where ever it happens to take you. I would like you, on some level,

[DJ's hand raises.]

That's right–to make one note of something about this space that you're going to. And as you make that one note of the space that you're going to, this border, this edge, whatever it happens to be, as your arm and hand stretch for the ceiling as you get to that place. When I count to three and you drop your hand and arm, and go a little bit more completely into trance. Let your unconscious mind share one or two words about that place, at that edge.

One-two-three. *Snap!*

DJ: [Dimly.] Vantage point.

LA: And deeper still. And then half way up on three. And then twice as deep when I snap. One-two-three. Awake. And *Snap!*, down again. And then deeper. *Snap!* and deeper *Snap!* and deeper *Snap!* and deeper. *Snap!*

And wide awake now! *Snap!*

[Slight pause.] and deep sleep.

That's right. I wonder if that feels like an express elevator, or a microwave. Just boom! Bringing something right there. Like teleportation for your mind. Deeper and deeper, now, now, now, now, now, now. Down. *Snap!*

Giving in to every little bit of that. Halfway up on three. One-two-three. And then twice as deeply down now. *Snap!* *Snap!*

And then a quarter of the way up on three. One-two-three. Awake.

And deep sleep. *Snap!* Twice as deep. Deeply down. And twice as deeply down again. *Snap!* And twice as deeply down now. *Snap!* And then 85% of the way again on five. One-two-three-four-five, awake!

[Longer pause.] Hmm. You can still open your eyes.

[DJ's eyes keep shutting. Lee laughs.] Deep sleep.

Twice as deeply down.

And then on twenty let your unconscious mind bring you back as clearly as consciously as alertly as possible.

One. Two. Three. Four. Five. Coming up. Six. Seven. Knowing how good it will feel to return when you can. Eight. Nine. Ten. Eleven. Letting everything clear. Letting your mind get more and more capable and able of doing other things. Twelve, thirteen. Fourteen. Fifteen. Sixteen. Seventeen. Eighteen. Nineteen. And twenty. Wide awake.

[DJ looks groggy. And groans.]

So how do you feel?

DJ:    I feel great. I do feel like I've been on a roller coaster.

LA:    What do you remember?

DJ:    Going up and down a lot.

LA:    Anything else?

DJ:    You sent me… out? To a different place. But I got nothing.

LA:    I asked your unconscious to take you to an edge of your mind. And I asked you to tell me a couple of words about that place. And the words you said were "Vantage Point."

DJ:    Oh, cool!

LA:    [Laughs.]

DJ:    OK, yes.

LA:   So you remember that you said it since I said it, but did you remember it before?

DJ:   I had a vague recollection of it. Like I couldn't tell if it was from a dream, or if that actually happened. It felt like a dream.

LA:   I still feel like we're doing this in kind of a compressed fashion. When Elman did it, it was for pain management. So we're doing it for amnesia, and I'm wondering if the amount of time and the depth of trance, if, instead of doing it for ten minutes, we should do it for twenty or thirty or forty minutes and see if... you know. But that might be an experience that we have as a total separate thing. So let's just take half an hour and just see how deeply into trance you can go with fractionation and see how much of that you remember.

DJ:   Right.

### Notes

DJ    Generally speaking I can see how some time spent fractioning would result in outright amnesia. I don't think that the time we did spend was quite enough. I felt like I could remember what was said, but it did feel like trying to access the time I spent in the trance was becoming like trying to move through molasses. The longer we spent going up and down, the more 'thick' the memories seemed to become.

# CHAPTER TWENTY-SIX

## *Experiment 26 Teflon-Coated Mind*

**New info slides off**
**Slippery feels amazing**
**Thoughts gone down the pan**

**The hooks entrap the**
**loops of your thoughts and give peace**
**Your knowledge is there**

Most people know about Teflon cookware. It is used to coat pots and pans so that food doesn't stick to the cookery. It is also a very convenient metaphor for a certain type of amnesia. In this case, the subject is given a "Teflon" trigger, which means that the new memories simply slide off the mind for the duration of the trigger. The subject can act as if they normally would, but anything that happens while the trigger is active simply does not take root in the mind.

It's an extremely effective trigger, especially for subjects who are kinesthetic learners (or, in this case, un-learners) and with strong imaginations. It was also effective on DJ, as we'll see here:

[Sound of typing. DJ reaches for a bottle of water. Suddenly—]

LA   DJ, deep sleep! *Snap!* Whatever you were reaching for you can hold on to that and remember to do it as soon as you wake up, but in the meantime, down, down, down, down, down, you go. Effortlessly, sinking further, feeling so very good about that. Notice how amazing it becomes, as you get really, really comfy. We're going to head back to that "Control Room"of yours and as we head back to that "Control Room"of yours, the same warnings apply. You're going to find that room, you're going to go in

178

to it. You're going to know that we'll do stuff that is only good, and safe, and fun. Even if it's a little edgy; still good, and safe, and fun.

And while we're here, somewhere in there, I don't know if it's on your memory panel or not, but go ahead and find this thing. And in the meantime, Forget Switch On.

But you're going to find this thing. Maybe it's on your memory panel. And it's basically says something along the lines of, "Teflon Conscious Mind." And just turn it from... Just enable that switch. It probably says "disengaged." So just "enable" that switch.

So basically, this is how it's going to work: If I enable the "Teflon," it's going to feel to your conscious mind as though the things I say slide right off it. No matter what it is that I happen to say to you while you're conscious, when that switch is on, those things simply slide right off your mind. There's no place for them to stick in your conscious self at all. None of that. And so that information can slide right off your conscious mind right into your unconscious, and your unconscious can hold on to it in the most neutral way possible. But because I think it's important sometimes to allow you to hold on to information, let's also give you another switch.

Let's enable the "Velcro" in your mind. And what this will do, when that's enabled, when that's activated—you'll enable both of them, whether "Teflon Activated" or "Deactivated," and "Velcro Activated," or "Deactivated."

The "Velcro" in your mind will give you a totally different experience on a conscious level. It will allow you to hold onto and retain information so that you can easily access it. Like if you covered your office wall in Velcro and you could put all the important things in the places where you would see them and they would always be there and most obvious for you. If something becomes unimportant for you, then you can remove it, and that space could be available again. But in the meantime, as your unconscious mind has just paid attention to everything I've said.

It has enabled the "Teflon Mind" and the "Velcro Mind." And it understands that "Activate Teflon," "Deactivate Teflon," "Activate Velcro Mind," "Deactivate Velcro Mind," is exactly how this works and you agree to make this happen, go ahead and reach out and push that green "Activate" button that lights up. And go ahead and walk over to that door and again, "Are you sure you want to 'Activate' say yes or no?" Go ahead and say "Yes" or "No" out loud and the door will open.

DJ: Yes.

LA: Thank you. And Forget Switch Off.

Go ahead and find yourself going down that corridor and, this time, find yourself walking all the way to ten and wide awake on ten. One, two, three–remembering what you were about to do–four, five, six, seven–feeling great–eight, nine, and ten! *Snap!* Wide awake.

[DJ takes the water bottle that had been in his hand and starts drinking it.]

LA: So how was that?

DJ: How was what?

LA: [Laughs.] Yes! [Does a little dance.]

DJ: [Laughs.] Oh dear.

LA: So, I thought I would do something interesting. I put you into a trance. And then I turned your "Forget Switch…" [Laughs.] into that 'On' position. And then I did the "Teflon" and the "Velcro."

DJ: … You did, did you?

LA: I did.

DJ: That's awesome.

LA: [Laughs, clears throat.] I did.

And I also had your unconscious mind hold on to what you were about to do, so I interrupted you in the middle of something, and then I had you go back to finishing it up.

DJ: Right.

LA: Yes. And so I think, that's a combination of techniques?

DJ: That is a combination, yes it is.

LA: But clearly something worked really well right there.

DJ: [Sounding mystified.] Yes it…

[Lee takes a drink of water.]

LA: Yes it did.

DJ:   Did.

[Both laugh.]

DJ:   Not that you enjoy taunting people.

LA:   Just a little.

DJ:   Yeah, just a…

[Lee drinks again.]

Little… You're such a tease.

LA:   It's true; I am. I love it, I can't help it. You'll just have to suck it up.

DJ:   [Laughs.]

One thing I like about hypnosis is, if the opportunity presents itself, at one of these weekends, I would just love to co-top with you. Because it would be so much fun.

LA:   I'm sure we can find someone who would be happy.

If I could dress up like the TARDIS I would.

DJ:   [Laughs.] Oh…

You know there are TARDIS corsets…

[Corset discussions.]

LA:   I think that went pretty well.

And just because you don't know about one doesn't mean it didn't happen.

DJ:   I know. The notes tonight will be interesting.

"So Lee tells me this happened."

LA:   So how about if I tell you right now that your unconscious mind let your conscious self remember everything that we did *Snap!* right now!

DJ:   OK.

LA:   Will that help your notes?

DJ:   It'll help my notes, sure.

I'm OK either way, and that's awesome. Does that include the previous part?

LA:   It included... oh sure, you can remember all of that, too.

DJ:   OK

LA:   Yeah. I mean... "For science," I don't really care. I mean, really, I'm apologizing to your unconscious for that horrible remark I made earlier.

And maybe your conscious self, too. I don't know.

DJ:   Yeah, yeah, well. It's funny...OK. That's really funny.

That was my unconscious saying, "Look, pal."

LA:   You should feel strongly about this, you should be angry!

DJ:   I'm playing along, but just know...I'm playing along, UNDER PROTEST!

LA:   It's good to know that *all* of you is firmly committed to that idea.

DJ:   And here's why it's a hard limit, even though it's not really a 'hard limit,' I didn't *say* it was a hard limit. So we can play with it, because it's good for our purposes, because it's not really a hard limit. But there's still a part of me that says "Look!"

LA:   [Discussions about DJ's team.]

Next time we'll do fractionation. Bringing you partially up and then deeper as a technique. And I think that what that will accomplish is get you into a very deep state of trance and we'll see if just the deepest state of trance possible will prevent your conscious self from saying 'oh, yeah, I remember.'

DJ:   Did we test "Teflon?"

LA:   Oh. Let's see. We can activate "Teflon" right now. And as "Teflon" is activated right now I can just say things like...? Let's see... What can I say?

I can talk about people never hit their thumbs with hammers whenever they do garden work. And... Um... see how well that actually works. And then I could deactivate that.

So... did you pay any attention to that at all? Did you hear any of that?

182

DJ: No.

LA: Ho… I guess "Teflon" does work.

DJ: And I was writing something, too?

LA: That's really fascinating. What did you write?

DJ: "Teflon causes a slightly altered state."

LA: Oh. Well. I would say that that's true.

DJ: It felt… and I guess because the feeling still lingers… it felt… 'Teflon-y.' Like there was a thing right here. [DJ points to right in front of his head.]

LA: So, I didn't actually describe "Teflon." But you and I both know what that is, it's a slick surface that nothing really sticks to.

And if I were to say to you "Activate Velcro," you'd probably remember absolutely everything I was going to say to you. And I don't know if that feels any differently or not.

DJ: Yes. People don't always hit their thumbs with hammers.

LA: [Laughs.] Oh. That's fascinating. Because it had you remember something in a different trigger period. Which shouldn't happen. It should be from that point forward. You know what I mean? But that's OK. Because we can talk about that, too.

DJ: [Still has his arms folded.]

LA: I'm not trying to irritate you.

DJ: Oh. Well… you're succeeding beyond your wildest dreams.

I am completely fine. [Laughs.]

Part of the fun of this is…

LA: That it's fun.

DJ: Is that it's fun. Look, part of the fun of this book is to show the fun that both the hypnotist and the subject can have. Right?

LA: Yeah.

DJ: You as a self-identified sadist… I assume that's at least partially how you self-identify. You like teasing, you like taunting.

LA:   Yes, I do. I like all of those things.

DJ:   You're a reaction junkie. So, if we're not demonstrating how it's fun for someone like you, an irritating taunt-y person, then… we need to get both sides of it.

So, as a guinea pig for these purposes, I'm OK being taunted and irritated.

LA:   OK, but the thing that concerns me is that "Velcro" shouldn't undo "Teflon."

You will hold on to stuff that is important to you.

DJ:   OK. Because my brain interpreted it as…

LA:   It's not an undo of the "Teflon"—they're separate.

DJ:   Because that's how my brain interpreted it. Once that switch was flipped, my brain will draw in what just slid off the "Teflon."

LA:   Ah. No. But it's fine if you did, for right now. [Laughs.] For right now.

I'll write that down. We'll find all the loopholes and then we extinguish them one by one.

DJ:   You say it like that, it makes it sound kind of sexy.

LA:   [Laughs.]

Isn't it really great that your mind is really good at holding on to all the stuff it could find useful?

DJ:   Oh yes.

LA:   I think it's wonderful.

So if I hadn't said that, and I just said "Velcro Deactivate." I wonder if you would have forgotten that you remembered. I don't know. We've gone beyond that point anyway.

DJ:   No. Because, at this point, my brain actually wants to play with it, and is having me forget whatever it was that we were talking about.

LA:   Oh, no, no. It can remember. It's fine.

DJ:   I know; I can. But…

LA:   It doesn't want to. [Laughs.]

DJ:   And because it got it wrong.

LA:   Well, it was a miscommunication. So we're just clarifying it, so that's fine. Those things are really good to know.

### *Notes*

DJ   I found each of these triggers very effective.

In the initial "Forget" test I have the distinct impression that I 'remembered' what had happened during the time it was activated, but that I actively didn't want to remember, and certainly didn't want to make the connection between my memory center and my mouth. Likewise, Lee's test of making fun of my sports team was the first time that my mind continued to hide her taunting from me, though I distinctly had the feeling that my subconscious wanted its displeasure to be noted, and then made sure that whole notion of me saying something about it was shunted aside, as if it were fading away in the rear view mirror. Throughout that experience, I don't think I consciously remember what the displeasure was about.

"Scopolamine" felt like I had been drugged. I felt somewhat dopey and happy, and willing to do whatever Lee was going to suggest.

"Teflon" felt like a clear sheet had been placed over my conscious self, and the words Lee was saying were just slipping off.

"Velcro" felt like an "Undo" button for "Teflon," as if all the words were brought back.

LA:   "Velcro" was initially meant to be a very strong "You'll remember this powerfully" suggestion, with the unconscious holding on to certain pieces of knowledge so strongly that it could always be with the subject as long as it was important to them.

In future play, DJ's unconscious also did not appreciate disparaging remarks against his team; I don't do that often. He consciously gets the sense that I've been talking about it, but generally not what I've said, if I use an amnesia technique before or afterward.

# CHAPTER TWENTY-SEVEN

## *Experiment 27 Elicit the Unconscious*

### *Attend, inner voice*
### *Muster all the aid you can*
### *Fun conspiracy*

Sometimes, after a subject has gained both experience with trance, and a comfort with their hypnotist, they feel that the vulnerable feelings associated with being exposed to their hypnotist fade away. When this happens, the hypnotist can pursue more direct avenues of communication with the unconscious. Up until this stage of the proceedings, Lee's communication with DJ's unconscious has been to ask it to indicate acceptance of certain suggestions by raising a hand to touch the chin or the beard. It's effective for gauging a simple question, but what if you want to communicate in a more open-ended way with the unconscious?

In this case, Lee asked DJ's unconscious if there were ways to improve the experience for DJ. Specifically, if there was something that would make things more effective. It's not a long transcript, but we present it as one way the unconscious can 'team up' with the hypnotist to build more effective suggestions, not just for hypnotic amnesia, but for other avenues as well.

Also, the answer does reveal a little bit about DJ and his needs and desires. Be prepared for such an outcome once the unconscious is comfortable enough. Also note, that it is likely this will not be as successful until you have reached that level of trust. As such, this 'experiment' is not so much a method of achieving amnesia per se, but a method of enabling the mind to be more comfortable with amnesia, as we'll see.

LA: I'm going to specifically put "Have the unconscious mind direct the conscious self do something the unconscious knows would cause it to have amnesia." Because I feel that that really isn't the "Fade Away."

So part of me wonders if you just went really deep into trance, and if that was what was focused on in the beginning of the session, how deep do you need to go in order to not consciously remember things. And the other part of me right now goes "Well is there a space in your unconscious mind where it can go where it doesn't remember things. Where there's a deep enough trance state, and, how quickly can your unconscious mind take you there?"

DJ:  [Long pause…reaches up and touches his chin.]

LA:  So I'm guessing that based on your response there is a space inside your self where there is a state that–whether it's deep or whether it's something else–your unconscious mind knows your conscious self in that particular mind-space isn't going to pay attention to anything I'm saying. It's automatically going to cause you to have amnesia whenever you're in that space. And, apparently, your unconscious mind can actually take you there very quickly, because it knows where it is. It can just go "Oh, boom! your conscious self is there, so we can continue to talk and say all these things and my unconscious self is paying attention and my conscious self is off somewhere else." So now that we know your conscious self is off somewhere else doing whatever in that right space where it simply forgets everything that I've said, let's bring you all the way back and get your responses to that. One, two, three, four, five, six, seven, eight, nine, ten, wide awake.

So that was really interesting, because that sort of a "What if?" and the "What if?" turned into a "Oh! Let's do this now!"

DJ:  …yes. It felt like a confusion induction.

LA:  Really!?

DJ:  Yeah. 'Cause …is it OK if I remember this?

LA:  Do you remember this?

DJ:  I'm asking if it's OK to remember this.

LA:  Yes. It's OK for you to remember that.

DJ:  OK. Thank you. There was a struggle there, 'cause I was like: "I want to talk about this, but I'm not supposed to remember this." Because you were saying "What if there's a part of your conscious mind that can do this? What if there's a part of your subconscious mind that can do that. And is there a state—it doesn't have to be a trance; it could be a trance…" so all these options were coming at me. That was like... "I should be in a trance... or not...for this? To decide this? Or I'll just go somewhere where my conscious mind will just forget that this is going to happen. Because that's where she's leading me. So I guess I'll go there."

LA: [Laughing.] I was planning on having a conversation, and that's not what really happened.

DJ: I am at that state... that's all I can say. So I think the answer is "Yes." Now, were you thinking in terms of...? I think part of it is... it... and I don't know if there's an mp3 you did, or if my brain is at the point where it picks up on these things, there's a part of me that feels like you suggest something, and my brain is saying "I should feel that." [Paraphrased.]

LA: Nice.

DJ: And wants to go there. So, that's cool and interesting. But, your question is–to go back to the actual question for discussion purposes–"Is there a part where I can seem conscious...?"

LA: No, no. What I'm really wondering is that... so... people go into all sorts of depths of trance, whatever that means for them. But is there a place within that space, where your conscious mind might go where it simply doesn't remember what's being said. And if your unconscious mind knows where that is, can it send your conscious mind there? So I wrote that down, I didn't give it a number, but I wrote that down. But I think that that is a simple way, maybe, of making that happen.

DJ: OK, so it's a variant of what we were talking about before, in terms of you telling your subconscious mind, "Have your conscious mind do something, whatever that is."

LA: It kind of is. Except it's more like, your unconscious knows that there's a space, and I ask, "Is there a space?" And you nodded. So, if there is a space where your conscious mind won't remember stuff, then go ahead and send it there, why not? Let's see what happens!

DJ: Yeah, 'cause what was happening was that my unconscious mind interpreted it as, "I'm going to send my conscious mind to go do something," and it went back to counting down numbers, and giving it something to do.

LA: OK. Because you know that's effective for you. For you, that's your space. That may not be the only space.

DJ: Sure.

LA: But that's a space where your unconscious is familiar enough to go, "Oh yeah, that's what's going to happen." So that's pretty cool. And other people will probably have their own experiences, whatever that means, especially if someone... That's kind of a nice thing... I'm listening to how it went, and I'm thinking that's sort of really elegant:

"If your unconscious knows that there's a space where your conscious self can go where it won't remember what's being said, have your unconscious mind send it there right now."

I mean, that's simple. Right?

DJ: It is simple and it is... there is something about those words—to me anyway, and I'd be interested to see how other people would react, because for me that is kind of trance inducing. Because you're giving... you're essentially saying, "Look, unconscious, you're in charge here, go, whatever that place is, you have full power, go for it." It makes it really interesting.

LA: That makes me really happy, because I like empowering the unconscious to do things. So, I don't know, on a lot of levels this makes me very happy. I'm empowering the unconscious mind, and the unconscious mind is doing something really cool. And it's doing something really cool in a context that I'm looking for, anyway. So, I like all of that.

[From a later session.]

LA: Wow. We're almost near the end; this is exciting.

All right. Deep sleep! *Snap!* That's right. You know how simple it is to find yourself sinking completely into trance, completely into that state where your unconscious mind is so very aware of everything it is that I'm saying and as your unconscious mind becomes more and more aware of everything it is that I'm saying and even right now while your conscious self is drifting away it might still be paying a little bit of attention to what I'm telling you. But, I'm pretty sure that that will change in just a moment or two. I'd like your unconscious mind right now, as you find yourself going more and more intensely into trance, more deeply into that state, and as your unconscious mind comes closer and holds itself, no matter how deeply into trance you go, at the very best level or place for you to find my suggestions as powerful for you as they can be, I'd like your unconscious mind to just do something.

Whatever it is that you already know how to do. That your unconscious mind knows will cause the conscious self to have amnesia about any of this little bit. From the moment I said to you "Deep Sleep," until the moment I say "Wide Awake." And as your unconscious mind knows what that thing is, will be, and agrees to make it happen, go ahead and just touch your chin, and let your hand drop down again.

[DJ does so.]

Thank you. And now, because we were talking about this earlier, is there something you can tell me which will make this more effective?

DJ: In general, or specifically now?

LA: Specifically now.

DJ: For right now, no. This has been so much fun.

LA: Thank you. I'm glad you're enjoying yourself. I'm having a good time working with you. So if there's nothing specifically right now, what would you like to tell me, in general?

DJ: I think me knowing the enjoyment you're having, as a hypnotist, is helpful. And also, for the control-freak that I am, some assurances that these things will be remembered later.

LA: OK. Well, I'm definitely having a good time. Hopefully you know that I'm having a good time, but I'll tell you again, anyway. And I'll keep that in mind. And I'm not exactly sure when you'll remember all of these things. But I'm sure there will be a point in time when you will remember all of them. Whether it's when you read the transcript, whether you listen to the audios. Or whether it's one of those times when I say "Remember everything," and then you can. And thank you again. I do so much appreciate what you are able to do with DJ, from my suggestions.

DJ: Thanks. And, actually, some sort of physical, verbal part is really helping me go deeper.

LA: "Some sort of physical, verbal part," what do you mean?

DJ: Somehow the act of talking…

LA: …makes you go deeper?

DJ: Yeah.

LA: That's really fascinating. There are a lot of people, well, there are some people, at any rate, who seem to think that talking brings them up out of trance. But I think that if that does happen, I think it's a function of fractionation. Because if you come up, and then you sink down more deeply, which is almost inevitable, unless someone is telling you to come all the way up, that you have the opportunity to go deeper. And I don't know if any part of you experiences that 'come up' at all. Or if just the act of talking, by my asking you to, might simply trigger for you that desire to slip more firmly into trance. Because, you know, we're all different. Let's let your conscious self find out about this conversation when we go through this transcript and when we go through the audio. If that's OK with you. Otherwise, it can remember we had a conversation, and it can remember bits of this. But let's let it be a surprise. Is that OK with you?

DJ: I think when I sit down to write the… thoughts later on tonight might be a good idea.

LA: OK. Let's let that happen, then.

DJ: [Smiling.] Yes.

LA: [Laughs.] Thanks.

So, go ahead and come back up on ten.

DJ: [Makes a disappointed sound.]

LA: I know… it's so good to stay where you are.

But this let's you go down again some other time.

One, two, three, four, five, six, seven, eight, nine, and ten. Wide awake.

DJ: …OK. I was definitely in a trance.

LA: [Laughs, gently.] OK.

DJ: Wow! [Pause.]

Usually I have some sort of vague memory of what happened in a trance. [Another pause.]

I got nothing.

LA: Do you want to read number 28 again?

DJ: [Reads, whistles nonchalantly.]

OK great. That worked just fine, then.

LA: [Laughs.] Yeah.

DJ: [Sighs.] And I had a slight headache going in and I don't have one right now.

LA: Even better. What I'm going to say is, go ahead and remember that now.

DJ: …no. I'm not supposed to remember it until later.

LA: Well, you can remember some of it now. But you'll remember the rest later. Can you make that happen?

DJ: Sure. Which part am I supposed to remember?

LA: Right now you can remember everything but the conversation.

DJ: You sent me really deep.

LA: Yes.

Well… sort of. I did send you deeply into trance. I will let you discover the other thing when you write up the notes later. And, you know, don't rush it, you have other stuff to do. It's your break time.

DJ: Wow. Like, seriously, a lot of the other times we've gone into trance, there'll be some memories, but here I don't want to remember, it's not there, I know there is a trance, I know have a 'yummy' feeling about it, but…it's so cool.

It's like it was literally… like you were talking about the other day… there is memory, and a bubble of memory that I can't get at stitched in there, and if I *really* wanted to get at it, I could. But… I can't right now.

LA: That's right.

DJ: [Laughs.]

LA: And we're both OK with that, just so you know.

DJ: OK. Good.

LA: [Laughs.]

DJ: OK that's so cool. Wow.

LA:   There is something really amazing about knowing that you're capable of this. And, when that memory does come back to you, that you're capable of that, too. And so, now is not the right time for you to know it, because when you learn it later, it'll be so much more effective. It's not like you're at a quiz and you need to know the answer this instant.

## Notes

DJ    This was incredibly powerful. In some ways it felt like my subconscious was saying "Aha! Finally!" When Lee was talking to the subconscious it totally felt like my conscious self was elbowed aside.

Prior to that, both seemed to be working in tandem; memories would still be lurking about, and it felt very much like my conscious self was being consulted (whether directly or indirectly) on any decision. When Lee consulted with my subconscious on the best way forward, I felt for the first time like I (speaking for my conscious self) wasn't entirely in control. This was such an amazing feeling.

If anything, I've been delaying writing this part of the session notes because my subconscious still wants to show off (I am automatic-writing this) and show what it can do. As a result, I still don't have full memories of everything that happened on the Saturday session. Did we do memory vacuum?

The two things that were required:

1) Reassurance to the top part of me: that the memories could be there if necessary.

2) Reassurance to the bottom/submissive part of me: have I been doing a good job? (Auto-writing again: I don't think it's something I'm going to need each and every time something is tried, but the subconscious wouldn't mind some occasional direct rewards/kudos, thanks!)

LA:   Since this time, DJ's unconscious mind has become far more active—and some of its activities are still hidden from his conscious. His unconscious self has its own Tumblr account, for instance, and occasionally talks with other people's unconscious minds (or my conscious one) about things which are important to him to do in that state, often scene-setting up and negotiation for future play.

# CHAPTER TWENTY-EIGHT

## Experiment 28 Memory Vacuum

**Metaphors work, friend**
**Suck all your deep thoughts away**
**Empty, like deep space**

If there's one thing we've seen time and time again as we've gone through these experiments is the power of metaphor. Whether it's "Teflon" or "Scopolamine," couching suggestions in familiar metaphors gives the unconscious mind something to hold onto as it attempts new and unfamiliar tasks.

One method used by Lee is the "Memory Vacuum." This asks the unconscious to imagine a vacuum cleaner that is used to 'suck up' certain memories and store them in the vacuum bag. This is useful as both a familiar metaphor, but also assures the mind that the memories are stored somewhere for later retrieval. All the hypnotist has to do is 'open the bag' and let the memories out.

Again, using the proper metaphor can be very useful and powerful, and it wound up being very powerful for DJ as well.

LA: DJ. Deep sleep! *Snap!* Down, down, down, down, down. That's right. In fact, why don't you let yourself go as deeply down into trance as you just were? I bet you can find that happening really quickly and really easily. That sense of your conscious mind level, that you've gone into a deep state of trance. Now, this particular trance can be remembered, but it still might feel really good for your conscious self to know how deeply in trance it is. And, in the meantime, I'll talk to your lovely unconscious mind again.

You've heard me talk about the "Memory Vacuum" before. And the idea of this is that it functions–on some level–like a real vacuum. But instead of picking up dirt and dust and debris, it takes up memories of something that just happened. And I don't know what your limit is for that, and that's OK.

Most of the stuff that we do will probably be fairly short-term. But I imagine we could either vacuum out an event or vacuum back *to* an event. And so your unconscious mind… perhaps this is an interesting thing, much like you were talking about it as a bubble–that's not how I see it, but if you see it, that's fine–we can think about the dust bag of your memory vacuum as being that bubble, that's floating around in your brain after you've taken that information, after you've vacuumed it up, either an event or back to some event.

And what your unconscious mind does with that is, put that in a bubble, and what your conscious mind will simply freely be able to move forward with this clean space. That clean mind, and in a way that, just like with dust and dirt on the floor, how when it's gone you don't notice it, you don't remember the exact patterns of where things were. You don't remember the particular spot, that little grain of sand on the floor, where it was, where you kept stepping on it. It's so completely clean and blank and empty. Let's include in that a suction to find yourself moving forward in time, with a drive to get on with new things. And as your unconscious mind gets that just tell me "Yes."

DJ:   [Distantly.] Yes.

LA:   Thank you.

And again, because those things will be stored in those bags as you call them, they can be released, right back where they were at any time. So hold on to that, in the most effective way possible. Notice how easy it becomes for these things to be good for you. Long-lasting. Wonderful experiences. Then on the count of ten, come back all the way, wide awake. One, two, three, four, five, six, seven, eight, nine, and ten. Wide awake.

So what about that do you remember?

DJ:   The…That was so cool. Uh…You talked about a vacuum… a, uh… a memory vacuum. But I don't recall there being a trigger. Or an approach for it.

LA:   You don't remember either one. Interesting. So if I was to say to you, "DJ, go ahead and memory vacuum back to the last time I told you to go into a trance." Let that happen now.

Don't you think that your unconscious mind knows what I mean, and can make that happen?

DJ:   [Brief pause.] Make what happen?

LA: Exactly.

DJ: [Laughs.] Oh.

[Both laugh.]

DJ: I see.

LA: [Laughs.] All right. Have that back.

DJ: Oh.

LA: [More laughing.]

DJ: Subject DJ is hiding his face.

LA: [More evil laughing.]

DJ: When you started saying "What if I told you"... It felt like my unconscious was saying "Yeah, OK. I got this."

It elbowed me out of the way. And something was happening.

LA: Yes. It's very good at paying attention. I mean, I don't know how much it was paying attention before. Because you've been into hypnosis for a while, but it's really thrilling for me to have the unconscious as an active partner. It just makes everything so much better.

DJ: It has felt a little bit like–and this may be a breakthrough for today, I don't know, it has felt a little like–my unconscious and myself, we're both always along for the ride together. And the conscious was always there, but it felt like it had to be a part of this, must be in charge, whatever. When, I think...

I was going to say something, and then I'm not supposed to remember it, so I don't know what I was going to say.

LA: There are definitely people whose unconscious minds who have quite a bit of autonomy and, even, encouragement, to do things with the body that the conscious self sometimes isn't quite on board with. And this is why there are people who talk about consent in that way. Because it's not like we're creating a separate personality. Although sometimes the unconscious does not have the same personality as the conscious. Sometimes they do and sometimes they don't. But, there are definitely–for example–there are some unconscious minds, I've read some reports about, mostly men posting about their 'girls,' that there's this other part of them that's really sexual, or really 'slutty' or really into this or really into that, and so they're able to use the unconscious to liberate those feelings. And the unconscious person will be happy to do a lot of those things, because for them it's liberation—really liberating to be able to go, wait, we have all these things inside of us that you, as our CEO, the conscious self has been repressing for a really long time, but there are benefits to us doing these things. We're with someone safe. This is an appropriate time. We should act on those things so that the conscious self can know that it's capable of doing these things and that everything is OK.

And also, you don't really need a specific trigger... Really.

But there are shortcuts. You know. It's like a control-c for copy and control-v for paste. It's a really great shortcut. And that's really what a trigger is.

DJ: As was proved today. I've been fortunate in that, I think, that I'm a particularly repressed person. So in that sense, I don't think we've ever really been at odds. It's a more a function of, there are these experiences that the conscious mind can't do without the help of the unconscious mind, so let's partner up and do that. I think giving the unconscious mind more free rein to do that, is more the experience I'm having.

It is a little strange to be talking about it in terms of–I mean, I can see how for... I hate to use the phrase "weak minded people"–but for people who don't really have a integrated personality, this could have the sense of being a multiple personality disorder issue. That's always struck me as something to be careful of.

LA: Right. There's one person I work with who's always had these aspects. They're all him, but they're different aspects of him. And sometimes they're more evident than others. But since we started working together, his whole self has started to be more on the same page and working together as a unit. And really, that's how we want to be. I mean, unless there's some sort of secondary gain, where you're not really able to express or you're not fully capable of understanding, I think for the most part, people want to be whole individuals and go forward with their lives and with the greatest of ease and the most confidence and our own personal power.

I mean, don't get me wrong, a lot of people willingly abdicate their personal power to other people. Some people have it ripped away. If we can give them back with a sense of...? You know, you could have been through some terrible, terrible things, because not everyone in this world is worthwhile and they do bad things. If you can understand that all of you is a worthwhile piece. And if you can get beyond the things that have been done to you, because they do not wholly define you, and they do not need to inform everything you do in your life, you can allow yourself to get to this point where **all** of you moves forward really health-fully. So you can avoid situations like that in the future. So that you can get a job in the future, or find love or peace or whatever it happens to be. I mean, there are just some terrible, terrible things. We should probably talk about using amnesia to get rid of terrible, terrible things and how we shouldn't be doing that. For the most part.

There are definitely ways for people to come to terms with the bad things that have happened to them. Mostly through a sense of disassociation and imaging what they might have done better. But when you just 'forget it,' those things get repressed and repressed, and those things start causing us to act out in weird ways. So I would say that that's something I will do a little more research into. And see what I can find for you on that particular topic. Because I think I have a couple of books about why you don't want to forget or repress bad memories. And it's not like you want to relive them or embrace them. You just want to accept that they happened and then find a way to either create resources or use resources that you've developed in that time to make sure that you'd be OK if the beginning of that instance ever happened again.

DJ:   [Laughs.] Oh. This is so cool.

LA:   So I think that worked really, really well. I think both of those worked really, really well.

DJ:   I...suspect that they did, too.

LA:   [Snickers.] You'll know later.

# CHAPTER TWENTY-NINE

## *Experiment 29 The Hammer!*

**Take all that we've done**
**Throw it all together now**
**Set to simmer; stir.**

When one is good, and two is better, maybe five is amazing? Here, Lee mixes and matches several techniques at once in order to truly overwhelm DJ's unconscious and render it incapable of maintaining a memory.

Lee calls it "The Hammer," and DJ is probably too far gone to call it anything.

LA:  So we've done bits of "The Hammer" already, but I think we need to do it all again. So, Deep Sleep. *Snap!*

That's right. Down deeper and deeper. And deeper down. And why don't you let your unconscious mind just say whatever it is that comes to mind. Maybe it's a random thought. Maybe it's just an agreement, maybe it's just that you're going deeper and deeper down. Maybe it's a "Yes," maybe it's a "No," maybe it's a phrase or a color or a smell that you have experienced or that doing that–and in between that–find yourself counting backwards by threes, from 762. Starting now.

And then if anything else pops into your head as you do those things, you just find yourself blurting those out. There's no real rush. And you can hear my voice saying those things with you right now. I don't know where you are now?

[DJ can be heard saying numbers.]

Seven-fifty? 747? There you go. 730. 727. 724. 721. Just keep hearing that as you go on and down and in. And while you're doing that, even while that takes you more deeply into trance, I'm going to bring you back out of trance about halfway right now. And next time you say a number, just feel yourself plunging down, twice as deep as you were before. One, two, three. *Snap!*

DJ: [Says a number and sighs.]

LA: That's right, just like that. And we'll do a little bit more of that. Up again on three, half way up, One, two, three. Right now.

DJ: [Stirs a bit and then plunges right back down.]

LA: [Giggles and laughs.] What happens if, while you're deeply in trance, and you're counting backward, you "Loop!" *Snap!* while you're deeply in trance and counting backward. Or perhaps you're repeating that number, or that same set of numbers over and over and over again.

And as you find yourself remembering to forget and forgetting to remember everything on that conscious level, notice how very good it feels, and how simple it gets. [Laughs.]

And let's make your mind, right now, come up again halfway from where you are, and on the next number, go twice as deeply down as you are now. One, two, three, up!

And then *Snap!* down again.

And right now, while your conscious mind is still doing those other things, have your unconscious self...

DJ: [Whispers, barely audible.] I feel so good.

LA: [Laughs.] Have your unconscious self have your conscious self do something that your unconscious self knows will cause your conscious self to have amnesia, over and above whatever else is going on right now. And notice how amazing it begins to feel, to be in a state of more and more of less "How much more less can you possibly have?" I'll bet you will find that you've forgotten counting. Perhaps you'll find that you've forgotten that you've gone into trance. Perhaps your unconscious mind can make that happen, too. And let's get you some new memories of this, because I was having laptop issues and I was late. Let's give you the memory instead of not having had this session. Of having gone out to play with the dogs. Or to do something outside in the yard instead. Think about how fun that would be. Think about how simple it all becomes. When your unconscious mind gives itself a new memory about what's happening during this time. Think about how easy it becomes. For your unconscious mind to be in that state. Of being in absolute and utter control of what your conscious self does or doesn't remember and in this instance, of course because our goal is to have you forget what's been done, what's being done now, what you're doing, at this moment, to remember something totally different than what happened. Think about how good it feels. And I'd like to do something a little bit reverse. Because I'd like you, on one level, to not remember any of this. And of course, on the other level–the "For science!" level, the "For the book" level, the "For your own fun" level–I want you to remember all of it. But I'd like you to remember all of it in a kind of reverse fade-away. I would like you, for the first five minutes after this trance to remember *nothing* of this. Except that all of a sudden, it's time for our conversation and when our conversation should have happened, that you were out playing with the dogs, or something outside. You can make up something that happened that suits you the best. And what you can remember then, instead, is that we just got onto this call. And then after five minutes, let these things begin to creep back into your memory. Each and every one of these things, including the fact that we did the elegant amnesia suggestion, and the memory vacuum, and now, of course, the Hammer. And everything else that we've done today so far. Find yourself holding onto them and know how good it feels. And to drop down more deeply right now. Deeper and deeper still. Feel how very good that feels. Let your unconscious mind right now take you to a place that's so very deeply into trance, that you'll know it only when you begin to remember those things as they fade back into your memory when you come up.

And go ahead and come back all the way up on ten.

[DJ lets out an almost reluctant moan.]

[Lee laughs.]

I know. You'd really rather just stay down there. And I just keep moving you really, really fast. I get it. And at some point in time you can find yourself staying there for an hour, half an hour. Longer. Nothing else going on than whatever's in your mind a few words that can take you places.

One. Two. Three. Four. Must be a little bit confusing. Five. But the countdown's still happening. Six. Seven. Eight. Nine. And ten.

LA:  Hi.

DJ:  [Without missing a beat.] Hi. So a couple of laptop issues, I guess?

LA: Yeah.

DJ: How was your weekend?

LA: Mother's day was an all-day affair.

DJ: Oh wow.

LA: And Saturday I did some moving.

DJ: How's it going?

LA: Slowly. It'd be easier if I were alone in the house, but I'm not, so. It'd be really nice to just have a few more people doing this with me. I should just hire a couple of people.

[Banal conversation about nothing in particular for a while, about what they did over the weekend, dancing, music, etc. At almost exactly five minutes afterward, this happens:]

DJ: [Stops talking as a memory obviously flashes across his face.] Wow. I'm having so much fun.

LA: I bet you are.

DJ: [Laughs a lot.]

LA: I wasn't timing that, but seems about right.

DJ: Huh. I was really deep.

LA: Good.

DJ: [Sits in stunned silence.] So... we've actually been on for an hour.

LA: Yes.

DJ: Wow. That's pretty awesome.

LA: Yeah.

DJ: And I can see the hour marker on my Skype right now.

LA: And you just didn't notice it before?

DJ: Yep. And the notes on my notepad.

LA: Now you're remembering it all.

DJ: Yes.

LA: How's that going for you?

DJ: That's going great. [Laughs.] So, two times, really deep.

LA: Yes. Something like that.

DJ: Something like that? Uh, oh.

LA: I'm not sure that I'm the best person to have conversations with people after amnesia, because I'm always curious as to where it's going to go. Where is their brain going to take them?

DJ: No. No problem. You rowed along.

LA: That's right. You row along, and I'll go where you go and we'll see how that works out.

DJ: Oh my.

LA: Just like that.

DJ: So that's "The Hammer," then?

LA: Well, that was *this* example of "The Hammer." I'm certain we can do that again in more than 79 different ways. I mean, I just went through the list and said, "Yes, that sounds great, let's do that."

DJ: [Laughs.] This is so awesome.

LA: Now I wonder what sorts of things your brain is going to find itself wanting to do. Really, your unconscious mind is really good at this. So when it gets a taste of its own powers and abilities, what more is it going to want to come up with? Which is an interesting thing. Something one of my other partners brought up was, who initially brings up the idea of hypnotic amnesia, and then who subsequently is the most likely to bring up of that sort of thing (hypnotist or subject). For me, it's the sort of thing I like to do. And I would probably bring it up with many people that I play with. I don't know if it's most, but many. More than just one or two. Because I really like playing around with it. But once you've experienced it as a subject, is it something that you want to do more as a subject, or that you want to do more as a top? Or, you know. I don't have an answer to that.

DJ: I'd be interested to see how that pans out, too. Because I think it's something worth playing with. You know, as we discussed, my attraction to hypnosis is very much the feeling of 'going deep,' and feeling of having my mind turned off, and feeling what my mind is capable of. So, pushing that some more sounds like a lot of fun.

LA: Mmmm. Fun.

DJ: As a 'Top,' because I'm such a service top, it'd sort of be like what would be helpful for whatever it is we're trying to do together.

LA: Yes.

DJ: Although, I did have a conversation with Autumn, because we've been going back and forth about Hysterical Literature

[Hysterical Literature is a video series put together and produced by photographer Clayton Cubitt in which a static black and white camera films a woman reading from a selection. The video captures the woman from the desk up, As the woman reads, someone is under the desk using a vibrator on the woman attempting to bring her to an orgasm as she reads. The effect is very erotic and extremely engaging. And it is arguably, even safe for work, since it is available on YouTube.]

You hypnotize someone earlier in the day that every time you read something out loud to them, it feels like each syllable is a vibration going through your body to where it's most sensitive just the way they like it then add a suggestion that your conscious mind will forget that previous suggestion. Now I ask you to read me something later, because I can't find my glasses.

LA: [Laughs.] Oh, the perils of aging.

DJ: Or, flip it, every word *I* read sends those vibrations through you. Or we set up a hypnotic suggestion that you will experience everything a person in the story is experiencing. And then find a first person story of a person riding a Sybian off the internet.

[Other discussion.]

DJ: Did we actually do the memory vacuum?

LA: Let's see, let's do a memory vacuum of the whole session one more time for today.

DJ: [Shudders a little, and laughs.]

LA: Yes?

DJ:   OK.

LA:   Well, why not?

DJ:   Sure.

LA:   How is that working?

DJ:   [Brief pause.] How's what working?

LA:   I think it's working pretty well.

DJ:   [Coughs.] What?

LA:   What time is it?

DJ:   [Notices it's an hour later than he expected.] OK, what did you do to me?

LA:   You know…

[Both laugh.]

LA:   I think you need to stop asking that question, and start saying "Wow, my brain is really amazing, isn't it?"

DJ:   [Laughs.]

LA:   I mean, *your* brain, not just my brain, *your* brain.

DJ:   [Purposefully stilted, as if quoting.] My brain is incredible and amazing.

LA:   The more you appreciate it, the more it will appreciate you, or do appreciative things for you, or something along those lines. I could be wrong about that, but it doesn't hurt to err on the side of caution.

DJ:   [Laughs.] Because it's one thing my brain doesn't do is appreciate itself.

LA:   [Laughs.] Well, **all** of you needs to appreciate your brain. Not just the unconscious part. The conscious part needs to appreciate it, and really go, "Wow, my whole brain, every little bit of it, even the parts that I don't even know about, is totally fucking fantastic," and so there we go.

So let's open that bag.

DJ:   [Exhales.]

LA:   So, to answer your question, yes. We tested out that memory vacuum.

DJ: Yes we have.

LA: I would say that worked pretty well.

DJ: I would say so, too.

LA: Yeah, so.

DJ: [Laughs, writes on note pad.] My... brain...is...fucking...fantastic.

LA: That's right. [Laughs.]

DJ: Thank you.

LA: You're welcome. Make sure your brain is doing all the favors it needs to do in order to make sure you get everything you need to get done, done.

# CHAPTER THIRTY

## *Experiment 30 Elegant Amnesia Suggestion*

**Some words target well**
**Others state their goal simply**
**These, are so perfect.**

Throughout the sessions. Lee was searching for a command or phrase which simply and elegantly directs the unconscious to have the conscious forget whatever was going to happen next. After trial and error, Lee finally formulated the following instruction:

"Have your unconscious mind find that place where your conscious self can go, where your conscious mind simply never remembers what I've said to you, and then put your conscious mind there now. As soon as your unconscious self has found that place, let me know."

Lee generally sets up some signaling device, either lifting a hand to the chin or top of the head if on Skype with someone, having the subject raise or wiggle a finger if in person, or to simply have them say, "Yes" or "Done."

*We did not record a session for this particular suggestion, but in many ways, the experiments just before and after this one are variations on this theme.*

# CHAPTER THIRTY-ONE

## *Experiment 31 Pretender and "Take-on" triggers*

***Like sense memory***
***You're absorbed in brand new roles***
***Curtains on your mind.***

One use of hypnosis is for what has come to be referred to as "Transformation play." In transformation play, the subject is convinced that they are a different person, animal or, in some cases, a thing. One way to use the transformation play is to have a person completely subsumed into a character such that the new character supplants the subject's memories entirely.

Here, Lee installs two different triggers into DJ. In the first, Lee implants a trigger that temporarily removes the subject's identity and has the subject 'pretend' to be someone else based on the objects in the subject's immediate surroundings. In the second, "Take On," Lee has the subject 'take on' the persona of a specific person. In this instance, Lee asks DJ to "Take On" the persona of the Doctor from "Doctor Who." As you'll read, although the experience was entertaining and worthwhile, it was not 'fun' in the traditional sense of the word.

LA:  So—Deep sleep. That's right. And see how good your posture is right now? So nice. OK. So down more, and more, and more. And just notice how good it is to get to that place that you know so well. So incredibly deeply in trance, perhaps you don't know it that well. Perhaps you can go to that place where you were last time, right now. Where you were so deep in trance, that your unconscious self knew it. And take your conscious self to that place, that's so deep right now. Notice how very good it feels to be in that place, so deep.

And I believe that place is also a place where your unconscious knows that your conscious knows absolutely nothing about what's going on other than how deep in trance it is, and how good it feels. That's a place you can go to now, in addition to being a wonderful place where your mind is so suggestible, and your unconscious self just makes these things happen because it has that capacity and it enjoys using it.

And so what we're going to do now–two separate things, really–but let's go about this in a slightly different kind of way. To do both that is. Let's do both. Let's do the overarching change first. So basically, this is how it goes. When you wake up you will have placed aside all memory of your current identity. And you're going to have to choose new details of your life. We're going to call this "Absolute Change."

So as your unconscious mind figures out the best way for that to happen for you–now you understand that this doesn't mean that the things that you know necessarily go away–but it's the things that make you **you**, that make you DJ, that make you lawyer, that make you husband, that make you things like that, go to that side, or put in a box or something. You can even label it. And remember that this is a temporary adjustment. We want to remember that we are not creating a 'brand new' you. We just want to take some things that you know that would be fun, maybe some other characters, or professions, and with what you know or what you can learn, about that particular thing, become something else.

Actually, there was a TV Show–I don't know if you ever saw it, it was a while ago–called "The Pretender." And the guy who was the Pretender was brilliant. But he was also on the run from the government. But he could be anything he wanted. And he could do it so convincingly, with such conviction, that everyone around him believed it to be true. However, in this instance, not only will everyone around you believe it to be true, but you'll believe it to be true. So let's give it a name, let's give it a trigger. We'll call it "Pretender on," and "Pretender off."

And as we do that, think about what that means, to have that "Pretender" come on. Notice that you're going to be able to do this pretty easily as well, because you're smart. And you absorb things quickly and you can go learn things about what it is. And in the meantime you might find that you become very good at bluffing. And making those things happen. Because I tell you you can. Because I trust that your unconscious mind has the ability to make that happen.

I don't know if you're going to have the same kind of voice. I don't know if your eyesight might be different. I don't know exactly how your unconscious mind will make those changes happen. Let's just say that each and every one of those will be able to respond to my voice saying

"Pretender Off" as perfectly as DJ will be able to respond to "Pretender On."

As you think about that, as you think about what that means, and how you'd make that happen, let's add in the other thing. So, it's similar, and this one is more like a role-play. In this one, you, as DJ, may not really know everything that's going on. You may be aware of the beginning and the end, all the stuff that happens in the middle, that qualifies more as intense roleplay, is based on a specific thing. So with absolute change with the Pretender on or off, your unconscious mind can just come up with something, or perhaps someone else could come up with something. And when I say somebody else I mean me or you at this point in time. But for example, to find yourself really becoming this character and you find that you take on that person's personality, their styles, their speech patterns, perhaps even outfits. You could do other things as well. But let's make this separate and special.

So, from now on when I—and only I—say to you, "DJ, take on... the Doctor," it could be more specific, it could be "DJ, take on, your dog, Spot." for example, not really the sort of thing we're into, but just so you get the idea. If it was something else that might be, say "Robot," there would have to be additional titles, and programming and things that build around that. But Doctor Who is something that you know very well, and it's something that you can make that happen on your own. If it was your dog, and you know Spot much better than I do, so you could probably do that sort of thing (meaning the subject can know all they need to know to make this transformation happen), too. If it was something more specific like robot play, and you were unfamiliar with what a robot does, or, what the hypnotist would want their robot to do, after "Take on, robot," maybe a specific robot, there would be more detailed instructions and information that went along with that. Again, at the end, it would be "Take off." These all can be programmed, so it could be "Pretender on," for an hour. Or, "Take on the Doctor, for the rest of the night." for example. And as you think about how these two things are similar, notice how these two things are also different. One of them has a prescribed set of things you need to do, and the other is your brain coming up with ways in which whatever new identity it happens to be, whatever it is that you've chosen, your unconscious can just choose it. Is it random? Probably not completely random. You're going to base it on things you know, but you might base it on things that are so far out, so different. Maybe one of your characters is—I don't know—maybe the pool boy that was there the other day. Maybe one of your characters is a person that you've seen on tv. Or someone at work that you've had interactions with. Maybe it's a different type of profession, or a different age. So there are two separate things we're talking about, and I know your brain gets both of them. Let's bring you up on five, and see how they go. On five, your unconscious can simply turn the Pretender on for, let's say five minutes, and we'll see how that goes. And maybe we'll do the other one, and maybe we'll see how that goes too. So wide awake on five. One, two, three, four, five.

DJ:   Hello.

LA:   How are you?

DJ:   I'm good, how are you?

LA:   I'm good.

      So who are you?

DJ:   Ah. Very good question. Um. Well... I think... yes.

      Well, I'm [Daniel], and I'm here to do an article on interesting people in the internet.

LA:   Oh, really?

DJ:   Yes. Aren't you interesting?

      [Note: DJ's voice throughout this section has changed somewhat, becoming slightly more assertive.]

LA:   I wouldn't think of myself as that.

DJ:   Really? Hmm. Well, you are the person with the website who enjoys playing with people's minds, I think that's pretty interesting.

LA:   That's fair enough.

DJ:   So, do you mind if I ask you a few questions?

LA:   Go right ahead.

DJ:   So, what got you involved in the process of not just hypnotizing people, because I think I read on your website about that, but putting together something where you were selling items on the internet.

LA:   Sometime after I had been doing hypnosis for a while, I was on my way out to Chicago with some friends, it was a May, about four years ago, and I had all my stuff all packed, and they did not have their stuff all packed. I was at their house, walking around with my recorder and I decided I would record *something*. So I recorded this audio which I then called "Lazy Summer Day" while I walked around. Then I started to make other audios and other audios and other audios. Initially my website had a link to an audio on it. And then there were more, and then there were even more. Then lots of people said, "You should sell these." And I said, "…OK." Because they clearly wanted to buy something.

[As Lee is talking, DJ is taking copious notes.]

LA: So I started to create things that people could buy. I went through several iterations of websites. I started offering video Skype sessions for free, every single Thursday. Some of those Thursdays I would have up to ten sessions a day.

DJ: That's a lot of work.

LA: It is a lot of work.

I was offering free Skype sessions for about six months. Then one day after about six months I decided that I could start charging for them for most days of the week, and then many people started buying Skype sessions too. I kept doing free sessions on Thursdays with the people who started out with me.

DJ: And, um, I've noticed that a lot of people in the line of work that do hypnosis services online for money tend to use things like Niteflirt, or tend to be on the more erotic, sexual side of things. You don't do that so much. Is that a conscious choice?

LA: I am also on Niteflirt. But I tend to think of myself as less erotic and more mind control-y. It's not that there isn't anything erotic about putting someone into a trance and adjusting their minds, because there is.

DJ: Sure.

LA: There's a lot of porn available; here's a lot of hypnotic content around that's overtly sexual. I don't feel that I can specifically add anything that's new or exciting to that arena, but I think that the hypnosis I do is different enough from everyone else's that it's worthwhile to have it offered.

DJ: And do you find it erotic, the stuff that you do?

LA: No. Although, every once in a while, I *really* get into what I'm doing in a way that is thrilling. But I wouldn't call it thrilling in a sexual sense, necessarily. I just find it thrilling. And it isn't that I don't do sexual things. I find it exciting to be able to have instant orgasms. I think we need more pleasure in our world, and I think pleasure is good for getting rid of pain. I think it's good for flooding yourself with endorphins and giving yourself a better day. I mean, you've probably all heard or said or experienced that whole "That person needs to get laid," kind of thing, because they're so uptight. And there's something about having somebody who's just sort of 'stress free' because they've had all sorts of orgasms, and isn't that a lovely way to be?

DJ: So what is it specifically about the mind control aspects of it that you find "thrilling?"

LA: Mmm. I think there's something about being able to take a fairly functioning adult, and–

DJ: [Breaks in.] And what am I doing?

LA: [Laughs.] I love your mind.

DJ: [Laughs.]

LA: What do you think you were doing?

DJ: [Pause as DJ looks at his notepad.] I'm taking notes for an interview, apparently.

LA: [Laughs.] Why yes... yes, you were.

[More laughing.]

DJ: Huh. Hm.

LA: I'll tell you something else that's really fascinating about that. And I expected that it would be the case, and it really is the case, that other part of you, didn't have a reaction when I drank water.

[Both laugh.]

DJ: Interesting.

LA: Isn't it though?

It makes me wonder, what you'll be next time?

And I think that sometime we should do this, and videotape it, so you can look at yourself.

DJ:  Oh, god.

LA:  No, seriously. I think you'll find it fascinating. Like, both the thing, and the "What the hell am I doing?" was lovely.

DJ:  [Uncertain laugh.] OK?

Did I seem different?

LA:  Yes. And again, it's not just the whole "I'm drinking water and you can move about freely." But the mindset was a little different, so that was kind of neat. I'm not saying it wasn't like you, but it wasn't specifically you. Which is pretty cool.

DJ:  A different facet.

LA:  Yes.

DJ:  [Pause.] I'll remember that in time, right?

LA:  You can remember it right now.

DJ:  Oh. How interesting.

LA:  [Laughs.]

DJ:  'Cause, you know, I used to be on the newspaper in college.

LA:  Oh, did you? So you're drawing on stuff that... you know.

DJ:  And I think I looked around at what was here to play off of. And I thought, "Notepad, pen, paper...eh, interview, journalist, let's go."

LA:  Sure. [Laughs.]

Well, I was wondering how you were going to take it. Because I introduced myself. You said you were Daniel, and, I think there kind of does need to be a spark. Like if you were just sitting in a blank room and there was nothing there, I wonder what your mind would come up with? But if you were sitting in a room full of toys or stuff, or, not necessarily *toys* toys, but stuff, like "Where would you go?" And maybe it would depend on the room you were in. And maybe, whatever your environment, you'd adapt like a chameleon to it.

DJ:  Very interesting.

LA:  Mmhm.

DJ: And I think a part of me did register you were drinking, but I was like, "I'm actually someone else right now, so…"

LA: That's right! Yes, so that's acceptable behavior.

DJ: Interesting.

LA: So, DJ. Take on the Doctor.

DJ: [A short laugh, different than his usual laugh. When he speaks, it's with a vaguely British accent. He is also short and very confident.] This is a hypnotic trance, isn't it?

LA: Why do you say that?

DJ: Well, there's only one heart. I'm obviously not a Time Lord.

LA: [Laughs.]

DJ: And there's obviously no actual TARDIS around here or I'd feel it.

LA: You can't feel the TARDIS?

DJ: No I can't because this is a hypnotic trance. And I'm sure you're a lovely person, but is this person doing it under consent?

LA: [Slight giggle.] Oh yes.

DJ: Good. Good. Glad to hear it. So… why are we doing this?

LA: For science?

DJ: Ah. For science. Very clever, very nice… and your intentions are hopefully OK with this person?

LA: *My* intentions?

DJ: Yes.

LA: With which person?

DJ: Whichever person this is that I'm inhabiting for the moment. That you're eliciting this trance from.

LA: They're perfectly OK with it.

DJ: Good, good, good.

LA:  In fact, they've done it before on their own.

DJ:  Have they now?

LA:  Yes.

DJ:  Well, that's interesting, I suppose.

LA:  In fact, this is probably the best possible way to have this happen. I mean, when you think about it, to have you there...?

DJ:  He's a *fan*?

LA:  Yes.

DJ:  ...well... fair enough. I am rather magnificent sometimes. But that's as may be.

Yes?

LA:  Yes, you are. I am in absolute agreement.

DJ:  Yes. Well. So. Now that I'm here, what would you like to do with me?

LA:  Well. Mostly I just want to make sure that, at some point in time, when you have other opportunities to appear, which I'm sure you will, that you find yourself being 'you' in the most 'you'-like way.

DJ:  That's what I do.

LA:  Well... this person is now you, so you see...

DJ:  So this person is eliciting parts of me, that sort of integrate with his personality.

LA:  Right.

DJ:  It's a Doctor-ish person, whatever this person is.

LA:  Doctor Who?

DJ:  Ah, yes. Very funny. I haven't heard *that* a billion times before.

LA:  Not that you haven't said it a billion times before.

DJ:  Ah! I... have never actually said it.

LA:  Really? Not once?

DJ: I don't find it that funny.

LA: Just 'the Doctor,' then.

DJ: Yes, thank you. The definite article, you might say.

LA: [Exasperated sigh.] Right. *The* Doctor.

DJ: Mmhm.

LA: So—

DJ: And the reason I asked about hypnosis, since I am a practitioner, myself, so, although it's helped by my telepathic abilities, so it's a bit more invasive than what a human could possibly do—

LA: But then there is the paper... That's clever.

DJ: The psychic paper? Sure. That's clever—

LA: And so I'm guessing, that at some point in time, the person you're inhabiting and who you will inhabit again, and they will have some interactions with other people who may themselves be inhabited by other creatures/persons/others that you know as well, so—

DJ: Oh. So, it's hypno-play.

LA: Y-yes.

DJ: Oh. Oh, of course. Now it all makes sense. Fair enough.

LA: Yes.

DJ: So you want to make sure that all of this is going to work again at a later date?

LA: Yes... Yes. To the most nth degree possible.

DJ: And beyond, perhaps.

LA: The what? Oh, beyond, yes.

DJ: Fair enough, I think that would be fun, I suppose.

LA: Now, I don't know, at the time that I sort of 'invite you in' that when or who or what you might be, precisely. I don't know if you, for example, would always be *the* Doctor, who would inhabit him. I understand that there are different regenerations.

DJ:   Oh…them.

LA:   Them.

DJ:   Well…

LA:   Just saying.

DJ:   You can't account for one's tastes.

LA:   True enough. You probably could if you discovered all the whys and wherefores.

DJ:   Or something. That didn't really even make sense. Anyway, yes, you're asking…is there a question?

LA:   I'd just like to make sure that you're OK with inhabiting and being the most *you* you can be when these future situations come up.

DJ:   …yes.

LA:   I know it sounds a little bizarre to put it that way.

DJ:   A little bit… A little bit.

LA:   Well, you can always—

DJ:   Gold star for effort.

LA:   [Rueful laugh.] No. There is no try.

DJ:   Now that's an entirely different thing.

LA:   It is, though it's still appropriate. I mean, you don't *try* to save a civilization, you just do it, over, and over, and over again.

Or you don't. One or the other.

DJ:   And your point is what, exactly?

LA:   Your point is that you're doing these things.

Thank you.

DJ:   You're welcome.

LA:   I'm sure I appreciate this, and I'm sure he does as well.

DJ:    I'm sure he does.

       Hopefully, in time, I will as well.

LA:    Yes. Take off the Doctor.

DJ:    [DJ's voice changes back to his normal speaking voice immediately.]

       [He looks a little bleary-eyed, and starts laughing.]

       That was fun.

LA:    Was it fun?

DJ:    Yeah.

LA:    I think it might be really fascinating to discover all these different aspects of yourself that are lurking...?

DJ:    [Laughs.] You mean that condescending asshole part of me?

LA:    Sure. Why not? [Laughs.]

DJ:    ...sorry about that.

LA:    It's fine. I mostly have thick skin. Well, you know...

DJ:    Aww.

LA:    Plus, I totally get where they're coming from and it's fine. Not all the Doctors are assholes, either. They are Time Lords.

DJ:    Yes.

LA:    They do have two hearts. They can regenerate.

DJ:    Yes.

LA:    And go through time.

DJ:    Yes...

LA:    and these are very special abilities.

DJ:    Yes.

LA:    They still have their failings... it's OK.

DJ:    All right.

LA: [Laughs.]

DJ: It's very strange.

LA: Is it?

DJ: Because it didn't feel like acting. I was sort of lurking in the background.

LA: Wait, it *didn't* feel like acting?

DJ: The couple of times that I've tried acting (which, let's not talk about) it has felt like, what do I need to do to broadcast this view?

LA: I have actually worked with actors before and I think that once they become their character, it's a whole different ball game. Like, if the director has told them, this is who you're playing, this is your motivation, this is, etc., etc., and they get that, and then they become that, it's so amazing to watch.

DJ: Sure. And there was definitely a thought process of 'OK, the Doctor is now here, OK, is this a regeneration? Let's check in. No. Only one heart. And I felt my brain going right through...

LA: All the logic, all the reasonings.

DJ: Yes. So... this must be a hypnosis thing, because frankly...

LA: "This is not my usual gig. Let's be honest."

DJ: Exactly. I'm sorry if I was insulting at any point.

LA: It's fine.

DJ: Sorry. I don't think it is.

LA: It's ...fine.

DJ: [Laughs.]

LA: Your brain will... you're used to the way I talk. So that part of you clearly just isn't. And that's fine. Plus I wasn't expecting to have to explain certain things, and, you know. It's fine. Plus, I wasn't playing along, really, I was just sort of, being me. And that's OK, too.

DJ: [Cringing slightly.] OK. Good.

LA: You're no Ninth Doctor.

[Both laugh.]

LA: Anyway.

DJ: Doo-dee-doo-dee-doo. [Whistles.]

It was fun. I'm thinking, "I'm being really condescending. What the hell?"

LA: I wondering if that's what it would be like when you do "Doctor" scenes. Like how interesting that might get? And maybe there are other aspects of that particular Doctor that are not always that way.

DJ: I hope so. And I will do my best to nudge that in a different direction.

LA: To look for some humanity in the Doctor? I mean, what number is he?

DJ: Well, thirteen-ish.

LA: You'd think he'd have some compassion somewhere. You know. That's all.

DJ: It wasn't that bad, was it?

LA: No, it wasn't that bad...it's fine.

DJ: I feel terrible.

LA: Don't feel terrible. Feel great, feel great. You did what you should have done; that's the really important thing. So...?

[Laughter.]

LA: I probably won't make you be Fido [the dog], because that would be really interesting. I'm not really into pet stuff, so. If you really were, for a two-minute lark, maybe.

DJ: I mean, it'd be kind of funny to do Fido as a person for five minutes, to see what she would do. Except I know exactly what she would do.

LA: Do you?

DJ: And we just don't have enough snacks in the house. We just don't.

LA: The cupboards would be bare?

DJ: The cupboards would be... I would run to the cupboards, I would grab all the crackers and just start stuffing them down my face.

LA: So you wouldn't go for Kleenexes, or something like that?

DJ: No.

LA: I've had dogs that have done that. They're all, "Used Kleenexes are better than anything."

DJ: We have a dog that will occasionally find a used Kleenex on the floor and start chewing them up, but for the most part, no. Fido is still into snacks.

LA: That's good to know. So those worked pretty well I think.

DJ: And I seemed different as the Doctor, too?

LA: [Very seriously.] Oh, yeah.

DJ: [Laughs.] OK. I hope never to meet that one again.

LA: Well, I mean, I think that this is a different Doctor than you were with Ms. Mesmer.

DJ: Yes.

LA: So that's kind of a fascinating thing as well.

DJ: I think because... I think the way my mind was doing it was, there, my mind was playing between Tennant and Smith, being young and playful. Not to be the "War Doctor" as such, because the War Doctor can be too serious for what we were doing. So I was trying to be somewhere between those three, frankly.

In this one, you didn't specify a number...

LA: No.

DJ: So I'm going with the Doctor who just found himself in this body and obviously something is going on, because it's not a Time Lord body and so obviously, "Logic, logic, logic, why the hell am I here? What are you doing?"

LA: "You've been called to serve a great purpose."

DJ: Exactly, yes. There was definitely the feeling of—

LA: Intrusion? Like you were being intruded upon.

DJ:   Yes. And defensiveness. I think if I was slightly prepped for–"This is going to be for a fun purpose"–as opposed to, "What the hell am I doing here?"

LA:   You know what? If you ever find yourself doing this again, you might have a sort of leader board pop up with "Mission purpose" kind of thing. And see how that goes. I think that might make it a little bit easier.

DJ:   For everyone around me. Yes.

LA:   Yes. [Laughs.] Yeah, but I'd be interested in seeing how that all exactly plays out. Make sure that I'm not busy this time doing something else.

DJ:   I did open up with "I'm sure you're a very attractive woman."

LA:   Did you? I totally missed that. I'm really oblivious most of the time. Did you remember? It seemed like the change, the pretender, was more of a complete switch with the amnesia, and it seemed like, as the Doctor, you were there sort of observing that kind of thing.

DJ:   Yes. And there was some point at which I was seeing myself be some kind of asshole, and a part of me inside was thinking "I hope this is done soon."

LA:   I think it's really interesting because, although we haven't discussed "What happens in Vegas stays in Vegas" specifically. I guess that would be more of "the Pretender," sort of, maybe. But not really quite. I think it's really fascinating that you can have more of the remembering, or the participating, or the observing, and they can all be so similar and not be similar at all.

DJ:   I wonder why that is. It depends on how you present it as well. Because I think you presented it, when we discussed it last time, as taking another role, whereas "the Pretender," was presented as, "We're going to take everything you are and put it in a box, and you'll be someone else for a little while." Whereas with taking on the role, it was represented as "You will become that person," and that had a sense of being behind the curtain. Maybe I'm feeding lines, maybe I'm… But "the Pretender" was definitely the feeling of take whoever you are, put it in a box, and you're going to be someone else for a while, whatever that is, "Go!"

LA:   Maybe sometime, when you have time, and you're home alone, again, it'd be interesting to see if you could be someone else for a day-ish, or for a longer period of time, and see what that transpires as. I mean, I don't want to interfere with your wife's life so that's why I say that.

DJ: Yes, yes, yes. I think she'd find it even creepier if she came home and I was someone else for a while.

LA: Yeah, so I want to be sensitive to her participation or lack thereof.

[Discussion of logistics, planning.]

[Later.]

DJ: I'm sorry my Doctor was a condescending asshole. I will work very hard to not have that happen again.

LA: It's fine, sometimes the Doctor needs to be a condescending asshole. It's a defense mechanism; I understand.

DJ: He was obviously intimidated.

LA: Yeah, that's what it was.

## Notes

DJ: In "the Pretender" mode: It did very much feel like "I" had been nudged to the side. In place was "DJ the journalist" and I was going to ask questions and get some answers. My notes look very much like they were from the time I was taking notes as a college journalist. I had but a dim memory of the period as "the Pretender," until I was told to remember. It did feel like I relied on the props around me to construct a journalist character, combined with some questions I was actually curious about.

In the "Take on" mode: This felt like I was watching from behind a curtain as "I" was doing the things. I could feel the logical jumps as "The Doctor" (who was very much the "me" if I was playing the Doctor) figured out the logical jumps to "I've been elicited into someone's hypnosis play." I felt very defensive, as if the feeling was "Well, what do you want me to do now?" Also, and in part because Doctor Who was the source (in part) of my hypno-fetish, the idea crept in that 'of course' the Doctor would be condescending about hypnosis, because he is an expert in such things. I must admit it was interesting how a good chunk of it was very protective of me, personally. I will also say that I told my wife about being a 'condescending asshole' as the Doctor, and her response was that she wasn't surprised in the least; I do have a streak that is very 'snooty,' in her words, and this was the opportunity to unleash some of that.

# CHAPTER THIRTY-TWO

## *Experiment 32 The Explosion*

### *A picture, big & bold*
### *Blow it up in your mind's eye*
### *It's forever gone*

Ideas for hypnotic amnesia can come from just about anywhere. This particular idea came from an article I read on effective marketing or, in this particular case, ineffective marketing. The article referenced a story about a television ad for laundry detergent. Towards the end of the ad, the camera focused on the laundry detergent, big and bold on the screen, and then… blew it up in an explosion.

Certainly the advertising executives who developed the ad thought it would be memorable. How could it not? There was an explosion, after all.

What was the result?

After the advertisement was released, and people saw the name of the product exploding in front of them, a curious (or, perhaps, not so curious if you've been paying attention to this book) thing happened: no one remembered the name of the product. The commercial acted as a memory wiper of the name of the product, and sales tanked.

Obviously there is something about having a thing or a word explode that had some visceral effect on the memory of the person watching the explosion, and it was something that we could use.

Lee and DJ were teaching our Hypnotic Amnesia class at MEEHU 2, and Lee, having read about this technique of what not to do when marketing, really wanted to include this technique even though they had already recorded every other book chapter and had just about finished transcribing all the recordings.

They hadn't had much of an opportunity to discuss this technique except in broad strokes. They were near the end of the class, when Lee started to describe this particular technique. Lee was very excited about demonstrating it to the people at MEEHU interested in hypnotic amnesia because in her testing, it was VERY powerful.

Lee asked the class for suggestions about what to get rid of.

The night before, DJ and Lee and a group of friends had had a fairly lousy dinner at a local Mexican restaurant, and Sebastian Steerpike, a dear friend of Lee and DJ, mentioned dinner. DJ and Lee agreed that that particular meal was one worth letting go of.

Now, by this point, after all the experiments that you have read throughout the book, DJ was beyond formal inductions for trance states, and Lee simply began talking about the meal, asking his unconscious to gather up every piece of information about the dinner, to make it really big, bright, and bold, front and center in his mind.

When he confirmed he was doing that, Lee had him let that image explode into tiny little pieces, and to be blown completely away, out of his mind. Lee, through experience, finds it useful to provide an alternative memory that is simple and logical for the brain to rationalize. To replace DJ's thoughts about dinner, Lee suggested they'd had a good time and dinner at a sushi restaurant instead.

It was almost at the end of the class, and Sebastian asked how anyone would know it worked. Lee suggested that he could have the opportunity to verify the effectiveness. Once the class was over, Sebastian came up to the front of the room where Lee and DJ were chatting with people who had questions, and when he had the opportunity, asked DJ about dinner, saying something like, "Well lunch has to be better than that awful restaurant last night, right DJ?" DJ just looked at Sebastian, confused, and was like "Dinner last night? What do you mean? We went for sushi, didn't we?" Suggestion, effective!

One thing Lee found particularly amusing: the night before, they'd all gathered in the lobby to decide where to go for dinner. Even the idea about how that restaurant was selected completely vanished. Oh, the Mexican restaurant did have one thing going for it, delicious pineapple margaritas. Lee made an adjustment later so that DJ got to keep the memory of those.

### Notes

DJ:   The explosion technique is surprisingly effective. To this day, you'd have to convince me that we did not, in fact, have sushi that Saturday night.

Even when, as usual for the book, Lee gave me permission to remember the events, the whole night still has an unreal quality to it. My mind still wants to think about us going to sushi.

To be fair, the dinner was not the most pleasant of experiences (Midwest-Mexican food is just simply, never going to be as good as California Mexican food; my food was late and cold and they got my order wrong; the service took forever) and I think I was more upset at a restaurant's service than I can remember being.

Nevertheless, the whole process of 'exploding' the memory still lingers. And looking back at my recollections of that night is like picking up shards of stained glass from the ground and trying to reassemble them into something coherent.

It is a technique I hope to use again as both a hypnotist and subject.

# AFTERWORDS
## *Final Thoughts*

### *DJ*

I've come a long way since Lee approached me, over a year ago, to work on this book. At the time I'd had some hypnotic adventures, to be sure, but nothing really prepared me for how much I'd learn about what my mind and brain could actually do. I admit that–looking back on it–I was a little scared. As I wrote in my initial thoughts, I had lived inside my own brain for so long, that the prospect of screwing around with my very perceptions–the things I thought kept me tethered to the world–seemed scary and frightening.

But I did it anyway.

The explorations that Lee and I have done have not necessarily led to some grand epiphanies about the nature of existence or made any radical changes to who I am as a person. However, in so many ways, they were the culmination of my own personal explorations of hypnosis and the world in general.

By taking the first steps that led to Lee talking to me about the book, I had already begun. By saying "Yes" to Lee's generous and unexpected offer, I took the next crucial steps.

If you had told me two years ago that I'd be leading classes at recreational hypnosis conferences, like NEEHU, WEEHU and MEEHU, I'd have thought you were crazy. And yet, I've done that and more, including co-teaching a "Hypnotic Amnesia" class with Lee.

At these classes, if there's time, we ask the class to break into groups and practice the various methods we've studied. I confess that up until the most recent class at MEEHU 2, I had not really had the chance to practice from the hypnotist end of things.

One person asked if I would work with him, and I agreed. I placed him in a trance and used the "Forget to remember" method to have him forget that he was wearing his convention lanyard, that his backpack had been next to him and that he'd even gone into a trance.

I woke him up and had a conversation with him. As I asked him about the lanyard and the bag, and then told him to remember the trance, I saw his eyes widen with surprise at the memories as they flowed back into his mind.

Somewhere, a bell went off as I realized that this must be how my face lights up when I remember something after one of our sessions.

I knew, for that moment, why Lee and so many other hypnotists are drawn to hypnotic amnesia. That dawning realization–that momentary reaction when the memories come flooding in–is so exquisite to watch. I can say that I am hooked, on both sides of the pocket-watch, as it were.

As we've gone through these sessions and experiments I have been extremely gratified at how much more facile and–paradoxically–integrated my mind has become. By going through this process, I realize that my mind can, in fact, do so much more than I thought.

I certainly hope you, reading this, find the inspiration to use these methods to explore hypnotic amnesia and develop your own ways and means to play and explore this field. But even more importantly, I hope you close this book with the realization that your mind–any mind–is so amazing and powerful. And that it is a resource that craves activity and play and work and expansion.

If you find this area isn't for you, I hope you find whatever it is that engages and expands *your* mind, and seize it and use it, to find your own unforgettable adventures.

Thank you for reading and sharing my journey. Please, go out and have your own adventures, and please share those adventures with us, and with the people around you.


## LA

When we started this book we had twelve techniques to go through. As we went on, there were more and more. Our conversations include some of how we came up with more ideas, so you can understand our process of creating new techniques. Often, new suggestions are a direct result of this kind of brainstorming conversation or just a light-bulb going off during regular talks.

Your process may be different, but however you achieve results–new cool suggestions, new ways of doing things–is valid. Sometimes our conversations on one topic were woven into another. We've included these and hope that it's valuable to you to see how one thing can feed into another.

We hope that you've enjoyed reading about and listening to our personal experiences with creating hypnotic amnesia, and that you were able to effectively practice/take notes to discover just how useful and fun these techniques can be for you and your partners. As you practice, the subject's ability to forget **and** to remember should get stronger. There are many opportunities and different kinds of techniques here, and as with us, you may find certain ones easier to use at the beginning of your journey, with others requiring more practice. Trust is important, as is communication.

We'd like to invite you to share your own personal favorite amnesia techniques and stories with us at hypnoticamnesia.com, and to remember to have a good time as you experiment with this.

# RESOURCES

List of currently ongoing Erotic/Recreational Hypnosis conferences and their first event dates:

| | | |
|---|---|---|
| NEEHU<br>http://www.neehu.org/ | Hartford, CT | June 11-13, 2010 |
| London Hypnosis Workshops<br>https://fetlife.com/groups/88358 | London, UK | July 15-16, 2011 |
| DMDW<br>http://deepminddarkwood.com | Western, MA | Oct 14-16, 2011 |
| WEEHU<br>http://weehu.org | San Francisco, CA | Nov 1-2, 2013 |
| MEEHU<br>http://meehu.org | Northbrook, IL | July 18-20, 2014 |
| Charmed!<br>http://charmedhypno.org | Baltimore, MD | Jan 15-17, 2016 |

Worldwide Recreational Hypnosis event calendar and other resources:
http://hypnation.org

There are many established and new hypnosis groups, including large and regular ones in Boston, NYC and the San Francisco Bay Area. Here's a list (available by sign-up on Fetlife.com): https://fetlife.com/groups/55155/group_posts/4346843

**Books on Erotic Hypnosis**

*Hypnotize your Lover* by Wendi Friesen    *Look into my Eyes* by Peter Masters
*Mind Play* by Mark Wiseman    *Mind Play the Study Guide* by Mark Wiseman

# Experiment 1: Forgetting to Remember and Remembering to Forget

For some subjects, saying "forget to remember and rememebr to forget" once or twice during the course of the trance will be enough. For others, using it frequently in the midst of your other conversation will be more effective. Other double binds you might like to use include "Would you like to go into trance quickly or slowly?" or "Will your left hand or your right hand rise faster as you go into trance?"

*Your Goal*

_____

_____

_____

_____

*Date*_____

*Results*_____

_____

_____

_____

*Hypnotist Notes*_____

_____

_____

_____

_____

_____

*Subject Notes*_____

_____

_____

_____

_____

_____

# Experiment 2: Let Unconscious Hide Information

We found the phrase "Let your unconscious mind hide [thing] from you [for Y amount of time]" highly effective. In fact, asking the unconscious mind to talk with you and to share information with you is a very powerful way to both get a lot done with your subjects–consciously and unconsciously–and for hypnotists and subjects to learn a lot about themselves.

*Your Goal*

_____

_____

_____

_____

*Date* _____

*Results* _____

_____

_____

_____

*Hypnotist Notes* _____

_____

_____

_____

_____

_____

_____

*Subject Notes* _____

_____

_____

_____

_____

_____

# Experiment 3: Mail It Away

Have the subject discover every place where [X] information is stored, whether in their mind or physically. Once they've acknowledged they've discovered all the information or memories, direct the subject to imagine them as ink, and pour that ink into a pen in their mind. As soon as that information has been poured into that pen, it's no longer any place in their brain. Have them write all that information that's been pulled out of their brain with that pen, and "mail" it to you.

*Your Goal*

_____

_____

_____

_____

*Date*_____

*Results*_____

_____

_____

_____

_____

_____

*Hypnotist Notes*_____

_____

_____

_____

_____

_____

_____

*Subject Notes*_____

_____

_____

_____

_____

_____

_____

# Experiment 4: Restricted Access Room

Remember: You're working to create a room in the mind which is only accessible by the unconscious self and the hypnotist. Subjects, make sure that you trust the hypnotist; hypnotists, make sure you're trustworthy.

Suggested Language: "This is a room where your unconscious mind and I can share information. That information stays locked in this room until I take it out. Your unconscious mind and/or the room itself holds onto the information—only letting me and your unconscious self in."

*Your Goal*

_____

_____

_____

_____

*Date* _____

*Results* _____

_____

_____

_____

DID YOU
KNOW

? You can employ this method to develop triggered behaviors using the unconscious as your ally. Create information inside the room that the conscious self is unaware of, and yet acts upon. The conscious self may begin to rationalize why it keeps doing these things, yet does them anyway.

_____

_____

*Hypnotist Notes* _____

_____

_____

_____

_____

_____

_____

*Subject Notes* _____

_____

_____

_____

_____

_____

_____

# Experiment 5: Sudden Wake Up

This one is as it sounds like—you may find it more successful for you to interrupt yourself after you've made the other suggestions you want to, and say, "Wake up now!" and clap or make other loud noises to surprise someone.

## Your Goal

_____

_____

_____

_____

Date_____

Results_____

_____

_____

## Hypnotist Notes

_____

_____

_____

_____

_____

_____

## Subject Notes

_____

_____

_____

_____

_____

_____

# Experiment 6: Interrupt and Resume

This behaviour is meant to interrupt the conscious subject in the middle of some unrelated activity in order to do something else, then continue on, thereby making the subject forget what they did in the middle. Nevertheless it can be helpful for the hypnotist to do something similar for the initial trance state-using a trance trigger in the middle of regular conversation. Using Experiment 5, and waking them up suddenly is a good end of that initial trance.

*Your Goal*

_____

_____

_____

_____

*Date*_____

*Results*_____

_____

_____

_____

*Hypnotist Notes*_____

_____

_____

_____

_____

_____

_____

_____

*Subject Notes*_____

_____

_____

_____

_____

_____

_____

_____

# Experiment 7: White Room

Place or lead the subject into trance, and–before you create any suggestions leading to post-hypnotic triggers–have their unconscious create this space for the conscious, which totally and fully engages their conscious self. Lee describes it as the white room, but you can make it whatever you'd like. Before you give suggestions to the unconscious while "in" the room, provide the suggestion that the unconscious will act on these suggestions and "hold on to them" even after the subject is awake and "outside" the room.

## Your Goal

_____

_____

_____

_____

_____

Date_____

Results_____

_____

_____

Allow the subject to create as much of the space as possible by themselves. Leave it vague except for the color, the comfort, the lack of windows and the sound-proofing. The more actively the subject creates this space, the less likely they'll be to consciously remember anything you say directly to the unconscious.

Hypnotist Notes_____

_____

_____

_____

_____

_____

_____

Subject Notes _____

_____

_____

_____

_____

_____

_____

# Experiment 8: Focus on Something Else

When you have the subject focus on something else, allow them to pick a memory which is as vivid for them as possible, relying on as many senses as possible—sight, sound, emotional power, etc. This allows them to be as engaged consciously in a completely different direction from your words.

## Your Goal

_____

_____

_____

_____

Date_____

Results_____

_____

_____

_____

Hypnotist Notes_____

_____

_____

_____

_____

_____

_____

_____

Subject Notes _____

_____

_____

_____

_____

_____

_____

# Experiment 9: Going Through A Door

Movement through doorways or entrances, and even turns at junctions can cause similar effects. Start out with a clear goal of something for the subject to forget—have them go through a door, to the place they're supposed to do something, then have them keep moving on, and discover whether or not they 1) remembered to do the activity and/or 2) had amnesia about doing it to begin with!

*Your Goal*

_____

_____

_____

_____

*Date* _____

*Results* _____

_____

_____

_____

DID YOU KNOW ?

These instructions don't have to be given all at once, or even while the subject is in a particularly deep trance. Consider putting a series of suggestions on post-it notes, directing the subject to walk around and through a building while having the subject peel the suggestions off one at at time. Keep safety in mind!

*Hypnotist Notes* _____

_____

_____

_____

_____

_____

_____

*Subject Notes* _____

_____

_____

_____

_____

_____

_____

# Experiment 10: Scopolamine

When working with hypnotic Scopolamine or other hypnotically created drugs, make sure that these are non-reactive with other drugs a person may be on, and only have the intended effects. Some subjects are highly literal, and you want to phrase things so that you have success with the suggestion and a good time!

*Your Goal*

_____

_____

_____

_____

_____

*Date* _____

*Results* _____

_____

_____

_____

_____

_____

*Hypnotist Notes* _____

_____

_____

_____

_____

_____

_____

_____

*Subject Notes* _____

_____

_____

_____

_____

_____

_____

# Experiment 11: Short-Term Memory

Suggested Language: "Have your unconscious mind find the place where it stores your short-term memories, and as soon as it's found the place where they're stored, touch your chin. Thank you, and will you–from [X] moment until I wake you up–make sure that your unconscious mind empties that short term memory out and lets it stay blank and empty until I wake you up?"

*Your Goal*

_____

_____

_____

_____

_____

*Date*_____

*Results*_____

_____

_____

_____

*Hypnotist Notes*_____

_____

_____

_____

_____

_____

*Subject Notes*_____

_____

_____

_____

_____

_____

# Experiment 12: Rewind

Suggested Language: "From now on, when I–and only I–say to you 'X, rewind' and some number of minutes, or 'rewind to' some event, your unconscious mind automatically takes you back there, and you start over from that point in time. Whether you're actually starting over or starting fresh is to be determined by you, your unconsious self, and your hypnotist, but your conscious mind carries on just as though that period of time never actually happened."

Your Goal

_____

_____

_____

_____

Date _____

Results _____

_____

_____

_____

DID YOU KNOW

? For some people, rewinding for an amount of time is easy. For others, rewinding to a specific event is more effective. If the subject wants to be good with precisely knowing how much time has passed, they can be trained to do so.

Hypnotist Notes _____

_____

_____

_____

_____

_____

_____

Subject Notes _____

_____

_____

_____

_____

_____

_____

# Experiment 13: The Harder The Faster

Suggested Language: "All parts of you will do what it takes to ensure that [whatever the thing is I told you] fades away, as though it was made out of smoke, and it just gets blown from your understanding. The harder you try to remember, the more that information dissappears. Let it fade away, let it go away, let it just disappear."

*Your Goal*

_____

_____

_____

_____

_____

*Date* _____

*Results* _____

_____

_____

_____

_____

_____

*Hypnotist Notes* _____

_____

_____

_____

_____

_____

_____

*Subject Notes* _____

_____

_____

_____

_____

_____

_____

# Experiment 14: Right Feeling, Wrong Info and False Memories

Suggested Language: "Take this piece of information I'm about to give you, and then spin a completely plausible understanding of it in every necessary part of you, especially in your gut. Then create the rationalization for this, in every single realistic way possible. When I give you the new information, find yourself firmly, absolutely, committed to that story, until I tell you to have the correct information back. Please, and thank you."

*Your Goal*

_____

_____

_____

_____

_____

*Date*_____

*Results*_____

_____

_____

_____

DID YOU KNOW

? For false memories, be careful to only do recreational/kinky things with this, and leave therapy for therapists! Encourage the most right feeling a person knows how to have and associate it with the incorrect information you want them to have. Get unconscious confirmation that the conscious mind will behave accordingly.

*Hypnotist Notes*_____

_____

_____

_____

_____

_____

_____

*Subject Notes*_____

_____

_____

_____

_____

_____

_____

# Experiment 15: Pleasure Overload

When we experience pleasure, **lots** of pleasure, it can prevent us from thinking about anything else, and that's exactly the point of this exercise. Remember that your subject needs to be experiencing enough pleasure so that whatever else you're sharing–information or a suggestion for future behaviour–becomes noise for their conscious. You may need practice, or what Lee considers calibration, to get the pleasure level just right. Or perhaps you can just have your unconscious create that correct level of pleasure from the beginning!

*Your Goal*

_____

_____

_____

_____

_____

*Date* _____

*Results* _____

_____

_____

_____

When we sleep at night, our unconscious minds go over and over important things we've learned in order to commit them to our abilities. You can use this information to share with your subjects so that when they wake up, they're even more competent with suggestions than they were when the suggestions were initially given.

*Hypnotist Notes* _____

_____

_____

_____

_____

_____

_____

*Subject Notes* _____

_____

_____

_____

_____

_____

_____

# Experiment 16: Confusion Overload

When you give suggestions, it's often very effective to tell three truths, then suggest something you *want* to be true. So try something like, "pay attention to the temperature of the room (how warm/cold it is), hear the sound of my voice as it talks to you, feel the weight of your body against the chair, and notice the way your eyelids begin to feel heavy." The more you incorporate all the senses, the more integrated and profound the trance state can be.

Your Goal

_____

_____

_____

_____

Date_____

Results_____

_____

_____

_____

**DID YOU KNOW**

If a subject is going into trance before you have them think of all nine items, acknowledge that they are, encourage it, and do one of two things: say you're going all the way to nine even though they're in trance, or acknowledge that they're in a trance and you're going to move on with a deepener or suggestions.

Hypnotist Notes_____

_____

_____

_____

_____

_____

_____

Subject Notes _____

_____

_____

_____

_____

_____

_____

# Experiment 17: Freeze and Loop

Suggested Language: "From now on, whenever I–and only I–say, 'Freeze!' to you, immediately stop in place, and your body simply stays that way until I say 'Release!' as long as it's safe and appropriate to do so. No matter how hard you try to move, or if you try to relax into a new position, your unconscious simply holds you there, where you were when I said 'Freeze!' as comfortably as it's able to. You are as a frozen object, unable to hear (except me saying 'release'), unable to see, unable to move, and content to be perfectly oblivious to anything around you."

*Your Goal*

_____

_____

_____

_____

*Date*_____

*Results*_____

_____

_____

_____

DID YOU KNOW ? There's a similar state, "Pause," where the subject can still hear and see, if their eyes are open. When you "Pause" someone who was fully conscious, you've already altered their state in a powerful way. Capitalize on this state to bring someone deeper into trance, and then build on it to get to "Freeze" if working step by step is easier for you.

*Hypnotist Notes*_____

_____

_____

_____

_____

_____

*Subject Notes*_____

_____

_____

_____

_____

_____

# Experiment 18: Forgetting Orgasm Trigger

Suggested Language: "As your unconscious mind accepts this suggestion, and knows you're going to find yourself compelled to drink some water, that taking that drink makes you have an orgasm, and how immediately after it, you forget it, and that all of this creates a powerful desire for more water, or whatever you're drinking, go ahead and lift your hand up to tell me 'Yes.'"

*Your Goal*

_____

_____

_____

_____

_____

*Date* _____

*Results* _____

_____

_____

**DID YOU KNOW ?** It's best if your subject has an orgasm trigger built-in before you attempt this—if not, go read Pleasure Overload Chapter (#15) and then return. If they already have it, use that trigger when crafting your suggestion—the effect should be very powerful. You can also use a trigger other than a glass of water, just be careful what you choose, and when and where you use it.

*Hypnotist Notes* _____

_____

_____

_____

_____

_____

_____

*Subject Notes* _____

_____

_____

_____

_____

_____

_____

# Experiment 19: The Collaborative Countdown

Have the subject start by themselves, and watch how they respond to the suggestion that they'll go deeper into trance with each next math-problem solution. Join them occasionally, but suggest that they hear you answering with them on **every** answer. This helps keep their brain even more focused on what they're doing and really helps other suggestions you make slide directly into the unconscious.

*Your Goal*

_____

_____

_____

_____

*Date* _____

*Results* _____

_____

_____

_____

*Hypnotist Notes* _____

_____

_____

_____

_____

_____

*Subject Notes* _____

_____

_____

_____

_____

_____

# Experiment 20: Mantras

Similar to the countdown, yet very different, a mantra can become a self-fulfilling suggestion, so allow the subject to choose one they like: "I am a happy toy, happy toys obey" or "Obedience to Lee is Blissful Pleasure," for example. Or give them a phrase you like and want drilled into their mind–"When you hear my voice, you obey," "When I hear your voice, I obey,"–and then whatever else you say, the sound of their own voice saying this phrase aloud (or even in their head) is often enough to consciously drown out your other words.

Your Goal

_____

_____

_____

_____

Date_____

Results_____

_____

_____

_____

DID YOU KNOW

? With enough creativity, you can develop several related mantras which, perhaps, tell a story. Provide a wonderfully captivating spiral to look at and you can do some fairly intense brainwashing scenes. These are hot for a lot of people, so check with your partner and see if they're up for it!

Hypnotist Notes_____

_____

_____

_____

_____

_____

_____

Subject Notes_____

_____

_____

_____

_____

_____

_____

# Experiment 21: Dual Inductions, Multiple-track Audios

When doing a dual induction, it doesn't usually matter what you talk about. Generally speaking, the subject starts out by hearing both voices, then going back and forth between focusing on one, then the other, and then at some point giving up, and going very deeply into trance. Hypnotists can script out what they say to have their words strictly coincide, on occasion, or when doing this free-style, you may just notice that happens anyway.

*Your Goal*

_____

_____

_____

_____

_____

*Date*_____

*Results*_____

_____

_____

_____

*Hypnotist Notes*_____

_____

_____

_____

_____

_____

_____

*Subject Notes*_____

_____

_____

_____

_____

_____

_____

# Experiment 22: The Fade Away

Suggested Language: "Right now, pay attention to this information, '[X].' Then as you realize you have it, let me know by wiggling the fingers on your right hand. Good. Now, allow your unconscious mind to hold onto that information for the first four minutes after I wake you up, then simply let it fade away. As your unconscious mind knows that it can and will do this, wave those fingers again. Great, thank you."

## Your Goal

_____

_____

_____

_____

Date_____

Results_____

_____

_____

_____

Hypnotist Notes_____

_____

_____

_____

_____

_____

_____

Subject Notes _____

_____

_____

_____

_____

_____

_____

# Experiment 23: Esdaile State

You can achieve the Esdaile state with or without suggestion. For some subjects, you can get them there by waving hands or branches over them, or simply by taking them deeply into trance, then deeper and deeper, until for both of the previous suggestions, they simply begin to exhibit the signs of this state: spontaneous catalepsy, lack of response to loud noise, anesthesia, etc. You can suggest what the state includes and have their unconscious make those changes quickly, too. Getting to this state usually involves either time or an already adept subject.

*Your Goal*

_____

_____

_____

_____

_____

*Date*_____

*Results*_____

_____

_____

_____

DID YOU KNOW

**?** Make sure to give the subject some kind of exit notice, whether it's a forceful, "Wake up NOW!" or a specific touch.

It's a good idea to allow the unconscious to bring them up as gently as it can, but quickly, because they've been very deep, and it can be shocking.

*Hypnotist Notes*_____

_____

_____

_____

_____

_____

*Subject Notes*_____

_____

_____

_____

_____

_____

# Experiment 24: Forget Switch

Lead the subject to their control room, have them open the door and step inside. Remind them that they're empowered subjects and that this is a powerful place, so safety is important. Tell them whatever they need to implement your suggestions effectively is there, but let them create the space otherwise. Everyone develops their own images of what the control room looks like based on what's important and comfortable to them. Make sure you work with their ideas, and don't force yours on to them. Make sure you get buy-in to all the steps necessary to enable their forget switch to be "installed."

*Your Goal*

_____

_____

_____

_____

_____

*Date* _____

*Results* _____

_____

_____

_____

DID YOU KNOW

? When dealing with the control room, Lee gets the best and longest-lasting results when checking along the way that these changes are truly what her subject is looking for. Note the use of the "Activate button" and the "Yes/No" buttons at the Control Room exit. Also note that the subject is always free to choose either response, and that there's always a discussion about safety upon the initial entry.

_____

_____

*Hypnotist Notes* _____

_____

_____

_____

_____

_____

_____

_____

*Subject Notes* _____

_____

_____

_____

_____

_____

_____

# Experiment 25: Fractionation

There are so many ways to fractionate someone—bring someone up halfway, drop them twice as deeply down, bring them up 1/3 of the way, drop them down twice as deeply, bring them up 1/4 of the way, etc. You can also bring someone in and out of trance quickly, using different kinds of deepeners as inductions, speaking quickly, then more slowly (which can also bring about time distortions), and having someone come up just a bit when they inhale, and plunging deeper when they exhale.

*Your Goal*

_____

_____

_____

_____

_____

*Date*_____

*Results*_____

_____

_____

_____

**DID YOU KNOW** **?** Too many subjects get hung up on the precise meaning of twice as deep, or half way up. Tell your subjects that their unconscious knows exactly how much further up they'll have to go to be fully conscious, and can figure out all of those (seemingly difficult) math problems on its own, while all the conscious self has to do is drift away.

_____

_____

*Hypnotist Notes*_____

_____

_____

_____

_____

_____

_____

*Subject Notes*_____

_____

_____

_____

_____

_____

_____

# Experiment 26: Teflon-Coated Mind

Metaphors are powerful things—our brain processes information largely by
stories, by pictures, by translation. When you explain Teflon (if you have to)
or any other slippery surface, the subject's unconscious should get the idea that
nothing sticks, including their memories of an event, for the time you specify.

Your Goal

_____

_____

_____

_____

Date_____

Results_____

_____

_____

_____

DID YOU KNOW

? This is a good place to
begin playing around
with holding onto
memories, either with
the velcro or with other "sticky"
kinds of substances–glue, tape,
etc.,–when there are pieces of
information someone would like
to always hold on to.

Hypnotist Notes_____

_____

_____

_____

_____

_____

_____

Subject Notes _____

_____

_____

_____

_____

_____

_____

# Experiment 27: Elicit The Unconscious

When Lee communicates with subjects, she often tells them these two things:
1) I won't ask you to do anything I'm not 100% certain you're capable of doing, and
2) Your unconscious self can do most anything your conscious self can, often better.

When you begin the dialogue with the unconscious, it can return multi-fold results to both hypnotist and subject. To start out, you might ask for ideamotor responses like a lifted finger or a nod. Ask for verbal responses, then begin conversations with the unconscious.

*Your Goal*

_____

_____

_____

_____

*Date*_____

*Results*_____

_____

_____

DID YOU KNOW ?

Directly talking *with* the unconscious, as opposed to just *to* it, can make a massive difference in the effectivness of your communication. Interestingly enough, most unconscious minds also love to have their egos stroked—the more you praise them, the more they're likely to show you what they're capable of.

*Hypnotist Notes*_____

_____

_____

_____

_____

_____

*Subject Notes*_____

_____

_____

_____

_____

_____

# Experiment 28: Memory Vacuum

Create a place to put the memories, use the vacuum metaphor to remove them, and comment on how, just like the dirt isn't missed when it's gone, neither are those memories. Remember when the memories come back, all of them should fall back into their former places. You can also use the metaphor of a syringe to extract memories or information more specifically!

Your Goal

_____

_____

_____

_____

_____

Date_____

Results_____

_____

_____

_____

Hypnotist Notes_____

_____

_____

_____

_____

_____

_____

Subject Notes _____

_____

_____

_____

_____

_____

_____

# Experiment 29: The Hammer!

There are a lot of options when using the hammer—you can confuse, overwhelm, be direct, hide, let fade, explode, etc., or any and all mixtures of techniques you can remember.

Whatever you choose, let each method become more powerfully effective than the ones before it, and allow the subject to do what they can to remember after, so they can offer you feedback about which worked best for them, and why.

*Your Goal*

_____

_____

_____

_____

*Date*_____

*Results*_____

_____

_____

_____

*Hypnotist Notes*_____

_____

_____

_____

_____

_____

_____

*Subject Notes* _____

_____

_____

_____

_____

_____

_____

# Experiment 30: Elegant Amnesia Suggestion

Suggested Language: "Have your unconscious mind find that place where your conscious self can go, where your conscious mind simply never remembers what I've said to you. And put your conscious mind there now." Have the unconscious indicate to you that it's done so, then continue with your other suggestions.

*Your Goal*

_____

_____

_____

_____

*Date*_____

*Results*_____

_____

_____

_____

_____

_____

DID YOU
KNOW

**?** There are similar kinds of suggestions you can make. Find your own hypnotic voice, and discover what you come up with!

You may even discover that the Jedi Mind Trick–waving your hand in front of someone's eyes and saying, "You've forgotten that"–will also work succesfully!

*Hypnotist Notes*_____

_____

_____

_____

_____

_____

*Subject Notes* _____

_____

_____

_____

_____

_____

# Experiment 31: Pretender and "Take-on" Triggers

There are many ways to induce transformations. Adding hypnotic amnesia provides compelling reasons for the new person/animal/thing to be as authentic as possible, to take from their surroundings, and to let go of their preconceived notions of what it is you've turned them into. This may be one time when being precise as opposed to vague works in the subject's favor.

*Your Goal*

_____

_____

_____

_____

*Date* _____

*Results* _____

_____

_____

_____

*Hypnotist Notes* _____

_____

_____

_____

_____

_____

_____

*Subject Notes* _____

_____

_____

_____

_____

_____

_____

# Experiment 32: The Explosion

To ensure this as effective as possible, have the subject make this memory as big, bold, colorful, bright and front-and-center in their mind as it can possibly be, including sounds and feelings as well as the image. When they blow it up, it should disintigrate into the smallest pieces possible, then be blown away by the "wind" to ensure all the evidence of the memory is gone.

*Your Goal*

_____

_____

_____

_____

_____

*Date*_____

*Results*_____

_____

_____

*Hypnotist Notes*_____

_____

_____

_____

_____

_____

_____

*Subject Notes*_____

_____

_____

_____

_____

_____

_____